Shakespeare's Stage

The Swan Theatre, London. Sketched by Johannes de Witt, as copied by Arend van Buchell.

SHAKESPEARE'S STAGE

by A. M. Nagler

ENLARGED EDITION

New Haven and London: Yale University Press

*Originally published on the fund given to
the Yale University Press in 1917 by the members
of the Kingsley Trust Association
(Scroll and Key Society of Yale College)
to commemorate the seventy-fifth anniversary
of the founding of the society.*

*This book was originally written
in German and was translated by
Ralph Manheim*

*Enlarged edition copyright © 1981 by Yale University.
Copyright © 1958 by Yale University Press, Inc.*

*Printed in the United States of America by
The Murray Printing Company,
Westford, Massachusetts*

Library of Congress Cataloging in Publication Data
Nagler, Alois Maria, 1907-
    Shakespeare's stage.

    Bibliography: p.
    Includes index.
    1. Shakespeare, William, 1564-1616—Stage history—To
1625. 2. London—Theaters—History. 3. Theater—English—
History. I. Title.
PR3095.N34   1981   792'.09421   80-26513
ISBN 0-300-02689-7

10   9   8   7   6   5   4   3   2   1

To Erna

Contents

Illustrations

Preface

IN THIS LITTLE BOOK Shakespeare will be viewed
through the eyes of a historian of the theatre. A certain knowledge of the poet and his ideas is taken for
granted. Of course, we shall never lose sight of
Shakespeare the dramatist. But Shakespeare was
not only a poet and dramatist, he was also an actor
and a producer. He staged his own plays, appeared
in them, and, as a stockholder, shared in the profit
and loss of two theatres. This book is a study of the
theatre with which Shakespeare the dramatist had
to work. He lived in an age when the closest harmony
prevailed between literature and the theatre. The
student of Elizabethan drama cannot ignore the
stage. If he is unwilling to concern himself with the
workings of the theatre, he will do well to take up
Shakespeare's sonnets rather than his plays.

The attempt is not to offer one more reconstruction of the Globe Theatre, or to solve the problems
of the Shakespearean stage once and for all; the
available material is too scanty. It cannot provide
the bricks for a solid Tudor edifice, but furnishes at
best the elements of a kind of intellectual utopia.
My hope is to arrive at what Max Weber might
have called the "ideal type" of the Shakespearean
stage. If we can grasp this type, we shall have ac-
complished a good deal, perhaps as much as may
reasonably be attempted on the basis of the data
available.

The astute words of the classical scholar K. J.

Dover (10) * come to mind at this point. They might serve as a motto for this book: "The physical unearthing of new material is not in all circumstances more exciting than that kind of discovery which is ultimately the product of reflection, and a spark is often kindled by the mere juxtaposition of facts long familiar in isolation."

New Haven, Conn.   A. M. N.
February 1958

* Numbers in parentheses refer throughout to the Reading List on p. 112.

1. An Vpstart Crow

WE DO NOT KNOW what brought Shakespeare to
the theatre. Chance? Some incident in his childhood?
The story that he joined a troupe of strolling players in Stratford is pure legend. It is possible that
Shakespeare came by his first theatrical impressions
in Coventry, where the pageants with their scenes
from the life of Christ still rolled through Gosford
Street, Much Park Street, and Newgate. When he
was nine years old, the Coventry smiths paid a certain Mr. Fawston four pennies "for hangyng Judas"
and a like sum "for Coc croyng" in Peter's denial
scene. In speaking of the Elizabethan theatre one
must always remember this medieval panorama.

Shakespeare's first steps in London are obscure.
Legend says that the young man from Stratford
guarded the gentry's horses outside one of the theatres or that he started his career as assistant to a
stage manager—but there is no record of either activity. More likely, his theatrical career began with
a period of apprenticeship, followed by promotion to
the rank of "hired man." The first actual record of
his connection with the London theatre is dated
1592. Thomas Nashe's *Pierce Pennilesse*, published
in that year, contains an allusion to Shakespeare's
1 Henry VI: "How would it have ioyed braue Talbot
(the terror of the French) to thinke that after he
had lyne two hundred yeares in his Tombe, hee should
triumphe againe on the Stage, and haue his bones
newe embalmed with the teares of ten thousand spec-

1

tators at least, (at seuerall times) who, in the
Tragedian that represents his person, imagine they
behold him fresh bleeding?" This early work was
performed at the Rose Playhouse, whose owner,
Philip Henslowe, noted record receipts in his Diary.

The next mention of Shakespeare's success in London is to be found in Robert Greene's literary testa-
ment, *A Groatsworth of Wit*, published in the autumn of 1592. Only a few years before, Greene had
started out as a young man of great promise. Now he
was utterly exhausted and embittered. On his death-
bed he warned "those Gentlemen his Quondam acquaintance, that spend their wits in making plaies"
(no doubt Marlowe and Peele, and perhaps Nashe
and Lodge) to cease writing for faithless actors,
"those Puppets," "those Apes," "these painted monsters": "Trust them not: for there is an vpstart
Crow, beautified with our feathers, that with his
Tyger's hart wrapt in a Players hyde, supposes he is
as well able to bombast out a blanke verse as the best
of you: and being an absolute *Iohannes fac totum*, is
in his owne conceit the onely Shake-scene in a coun-
trey. O that I might intreat your rare wits to be im-
ploied in more profitable courses . . ." The pun
"Shake-scene" is obvious enough, and so is the par-
ody of a line from Act i, scene iv, of Shakespeare's
3 Henry VI: "O tiger's heart wrapt in a woman's
hide." There can be no doubt that when Greene was
dying in misery, Shakespeare had embarked on his
career as a dramatist and actor (*"Players hyde"*).

A bill from the Court accounts, dated December
26–7, 1594, links the actor to a definite troupe. In
the document Shakespeare and two of his associates,

2

William Kempe and Richard Burbage, are listed as "seruantes to the Lord Chamberleyne." At the end of 1594, therefore, Shakespeare was playing before the Queen in Greenwich as a member of the Lord Chamberlain's troupe, which had been formed from remnants of older troupes.

2. The London Theatres

BY THE TIME Shakespeare arrived in London, there were two tower-like theatre houses in the North End, the Theatre and the Curtain Playhouse. Information on both of them is meager. We know that the builder and chief owner of the Theatre was James Burbage, a carpenter who turned to the stage. The site of his playhouse was well chosen, for it was located in a northern suburb of London not far from Finsbury Fields, an amusement park. Since the Theatre was on territory under Crown jurisdiction, it was safe from the interference of the puritanical Lord Mayor. Burbage, however, did not own the land on which he built his playhouse, but only leased it. This later gave rise to complications that repeatedly brought Burbage and his family into court.

We know little about the physical appearance of the Theatre and still less about that of the nearby Curtain Playhouse. The zealots who protested from the pulpit against the "Venus pallaces," "sumptuous Theatre houses" and the "gorgeous playing place" are not to be taken too seriously. Samuel Kiechel (21), a merchant of Ulm who visited London in the autumn of 1585, was no doubt a more unprejudiced observer: "And comedies are given every day; it is particularly amusing to look on when the Queen's Men [a troupe under the protection of the Queen] play, but for a foreigner who does not know the language, vexatious that he cannot understand;

4

there are some odd houses with three galleries one on top of the other, so that a large crowd of people always come to watch this kind of entertainment." From this we may assume that the Theatre had three galleries. From other sources we learn that the Theatre was built of wood and probably polygonal on the outside. It is generally supposed that a platform stage occupied a large part of the uncovered yard. On three sides of it stood the members of the audience who could not afford a gallery seat. Behind the stage, but not necessarily as high as the three galleries, was a "tiring house." C. W. Hodges (22) has argued convincingly that the tiring house was not an integral part of the gallery framework but was merely attached to it. The "booth," a familiar sight to those who knew the street theatres, and the platform in front of it were merely fitted into the gallery frame, actually called a "frame" in the contemporary documents. The stage was probably raised about six feet above the floor of the yard, since this much room was needed for the operation of the traps. Moreover, the platforms of the street theatres were traditionally head-high. It was on this stage that Shakespeare played as a member of the Lord Chamberlain's troupe.

He also acted for a time at the neighboring Curtain Theatre. The name appears to have been derived from the Italian *cortina,* a space surrounded by stone walls, an enclosure. The theatre was a round, wooden structure, if Dover Wilson (45) is right in interpreting "the wooden O" in the Prologue to *Henry V* as a reference to the Curtain and assuming, therefore, that the play had its first performance

before the opening of the famous Globe Theatre. We
have only one eyewitness report of a performance at
the Curtain, provided by Thomas Platter of Basel
(5), who attended a play there in the autumn of
1599:

> They presented people of all nations with whom
> the Englishman kept fighting over a girl, and he
> beat them all except for the German, who won
> the girl by fighting, sat down beside her, and
> proceeded to drink heavily with his servant until
> the two of them were in their cups and the
> servant threw a shoe at the master's head, and
> both went to sleep. Thereupon the Englishman
> went into the tent [*in die Zelten*] and stole the
> German's prize. So in the end he got the better
> of the German too. At the end they danced very
> prettily in the English and the Irish style, and
> every day in the city of London at two o'clock in
> the afternoon two and sometimes three comedies
> are played in different places for the general
> entertainment. They vie with one another, for
> those that play best have the largest audience.
> The theatres are so built that the players are
> on a raised platform [*erhöchten brüge*] and the
> whole audience can see everything quite well.
> However, there are separate galleries and places
> where you can sit in greater comfort, but you
> have to pay more for it.

Although Shakespeare had probably played on the
raised platform of the Curtain Theatre, at the time
of Platter's visit the Globe had been completed, and

6

the Lord Chamberlain's Men had moved into their new home.

Platter also attended a play at the Globe, a performance of *Julius Caesar,* on September 21, 1599: "After lunch, at about two o'clock, I and my companions rode over the water. There, in the house with the thatched roof we saw the tragedy of the first Emperor Julius Caesar excellently performed by about fifteen persons; at the end of the play, as is their custom, they danced very skillfully, in groups of four, two in men's clothing and two in women's." The house with the thatched roof was the new Globe Playhouse, which probably had been opened only a few days before. The Swiss and his companions had had to ferry across the Thames, for the theatre was situated on the Bankside, south of the city.

What brought Shakespeare to the Globe? The owner of the land on which the Theatre stood had declined to renew the lease under conditions acceptable to the players. Cuthbert and Richard Burbage, sons of James (who had died in 1597), decided to tear their playhouse down and rebuild it on the south bank of the Thames. Peter Streete, a carpenter, dismantled the old Theatre and used the materials to build the Globe, which opened its doors in the fall of 1599. The enterprise was financed by a stock company in which the Burbage brothers owned half the shares, the other half being divided among the actors William Shakespeare, Augustine Phillips, Thomas Pope, John Heminges, and William Kempe. These seven shareholders were the original "housekeepers." But soon various reorganizations took place, and the

7

property was divided in a different way. Here it is only essential to note that to the end of his life Shakespeare remained part owner of theatrical property and that he derived a considerable share of his income from this source.

On June 29, 1613, the Globe Theatre burned down. During a performance of *Henry VIII* a cannon salute was fired as the King entered the Cardinal's house and a burning wad of paper stuck in the thatched roof. There seems to have been no panic or loss of life. One man's breeches took fire, but this minor blaze was extinguished with a bottle of ale. The event was celebrated in a number of popular ballads, one of which advised the actors to whore less and spend the money thus saved to construct a tile roof. Ben Jonson, who may have been in the audience on that fateful afternoon, later delivered a rhymed obituary on the house, with an allusion to the brothels situated near it. From Jonson's poem, *Execration upon Vulcan*, we learn that "the glory of the Bank" had had the appearance of a fortress; it had been situated in a swamp and surrounded by a ditch: "Flanck'd with a Ditch, and forc'd out of a Marish."

The second Globe was built on the same spot and was in operation by June 1614. Its outward appearance has been immortalized in Wenceslas Hollar's panoramic "Long View of London": a round edifice with vast "heavens" (erroneously designated as a house for "Beere bayting"). The new Globe Theatre was roofed with tile; that is, the third gallery was roofed, for the yard was still uncovered. Shakespeare never appeared on this stage, having retired to Stratford about 1610.

8

Other theatres in London competed first with the Theatre and then with the Globe. In 1587 Philip Henslowe erected the first playhouse on the Bankside, the Rose, headquarters of the Lord Admiral's troupe. In 1594/5 Francis Langley, a goldsmith, provided the capital for the Swan, also on the south bank of the Thames. In 1600 Philip Henslowe and the actor Edward Alleyn built the Fortune Playhouse in a western suburb, and in 1613/14 the Hope, on the Bankside, in a spot where there had long been an arena for bearbaiting. All these theatres were known as "public," distinguishing them from the "private" playhouses (Blackfriars, Whitefriars, etc.). In all public theatres the groundlings in the yard stood beneath the open sky, while the private theatres were entirely indoors and artificially lighted. We shall first concern ourselves with three of the public theatres of which we have more information than of the Theatre or the Globe. A drawing of the interior of the Swan exists, and we possess the construction contracts for the Fortune and the Hope.

The Swan was situated not far from the Globe. It would have remained one of the obscurest of theatres if, in 1888, an amazing document had not come to light in the Utrecht University Library. In 1596 (the date is not absolutely certain) Johannes de Witt, a Dutchman, visited London and sketched the inside of the Swan Theatre. The original drawing was lost, but a copy fashioned by De Witt's friend, Arend van Buchel, presumably from the original, was preserved and found in 1888 by K. T. Gaedertz. Up until then scholars had had to rely on scanty nonpictorial descriptions of Elizabethan theatres by contemporaries (chiefly foreigners); now a much more exact document was available. De Witt's sketch is still the only pictorial record of an *identifiable* Elizabethan stage. In his Latin commentary on the drawing, De Witt speaks of four London theatres (he calls them *amphiteatra*), largest of which was the one "whose sign is the swan" (*cuius intersignium est cygnus*), with a capacity of 3,000 persons. He tells us that the house was built of stone and that the roof of the stage was supported by wooden posts painted in such excellent imitation of marble that they looked like marble pillars. He had done the sketch because the whole had reminded him of a Roman edifice (*Romani operis*).

The copy of De Witt's drawing shows a platform stage, marked *proscenium*. Behind it is the *mimorum aedes*, the actors' house, or tiring house as it was then called. The space beneath the stage is open, revealing two stout supporting balks. The building has a framework of three galleries. The part of the first gallery closest to the stage is called the *orchestra*. The tiring house has two doors, which we shall call stage doors, and above it a gallery with eight persons in it. On the stage is a bench on which a woman is seated, while another woman is standing behind it and to one side. A messenger-like figure appears to be entering in haste. A trumpeter is in the upper story of the tiring house. These are the only persons shown in the sketch.

What was going on in the theatre while the wretched draftsman, who lacked an eye for perspective or proportion, was doing his sketch? I believe that a rehearsal was in progress. De Witt seems to have visited the theatre in the morning and sketched the interior while the actors were rehearsing a scene. This would explain why there is no audience; he himself was the only spectator. Who were the eight persons in the gallery of the tiring house? They have often been taken for spectators, because other sources indicate that spectators sometimes could be seen in the tiring house. I am inclined to regard them as actors or, at any rate, theatre personnel, who were following the rehearsal from the gallery and perhaps waiting for their cue.

Recently, Leslie Hotson (26) has once more identified the persons in the gallery as members of the audience and mobilized them in support of his fantastic theory that Shakespeare produced his plays "in the round." Hotson (27) developed this hypothesis on the basis of a mistaken interpretation of an Italian document regarding Court performances, and transferred the "arena" of the Queen's Court to the public theatres. I have elsewhere (33) proved untenable Hotson's theory that the actors at Court were surrounded by spectators on all sides. In any case, the occasional presence of a gallant or two in the tiring house cannot be blown up into an artistic principle. It would be just as absurd to maintain that Voltaire was produced in the round because spectators stood behind the actors at a performance of *Sémiramis*, making it difficult for the Ghost to enter. We have no reason to regard the persons in the gallery of the Swan as spectators, particularly since De Witt put no spectators in the other galleries or in the yard, where we might reasonably expect to find them.

11

It is only with certain reservations that we can take De Witt's Swan as a picture of a typical Elizabethan theatre. The Globe may well have possessed innovations or changes that considerably influenced the productions. And, after 1600, the Swan was largely unused; Middleton's *A Chaste Maid in Cheapside* is the only work that we can definitely assign to the Swan's repertory. De Witt's sketch of the Swan can contribute only indirectly to a reconstruction of the Globe. It is futile to think of a reconstruction unless some day the Burbage brothers' contract with their builder, Peter Streete, should come to light.

But we do possess the contract for the Fortune, which was built in 1600, also by Streete. The history of the Elizabethan theatre is a history of competing troupes. The Lord Chamberlain's Company, to which Shakespeare belonged, found its strongest rival in a troupe under the patronage of the Lord Admiral. Edward Alleyn, the leading actor of this company, and Philip Henslowe, a shrewd theatrical investor, were the leading spirits of the Admiral's Men, who started out at the Rose on the Bankside. When the Globe was erected on the south bank of the Thames and the Lord Chamberlain's troupe entered into competition with the Admiral's Men, Alleyn and Henslowe decided to build the Fortune Theatre in a western suburb, a new playhouse that would bear comparison with the Globe. Since Peter Streete had gained valuable experience in building the Globe, he was commissioned to build the Fortune as well. Streete's experience did indeed stand his new employers in good stead: they could simply request him to duplicate various features of the Globe. But what was an advantage to them is a severe handicap to us, for in the Fortune contract we repeatedly encounter the phrase "according to the manner and fashion of the said howse called the Globe." This does not help much, for we know virtually nothing of the Globe.

Alleyn and Henslowe could have said to Peter Streete: build us a theatre that looks exactly the same as the Globe. But this they did not do. They defined the shape and dimensions of the new house quite clearly. The ground plan of the new building was to be a square, its sides measuring 80 feet on the outside. The yard was also to be square, its sides measuring 55 feet. The space between the outer and inner squares was to measure roughly 25 feet in width and was intended for the galleries, of which there were three in the Fortune. The height of the galleries is stipulated in the contract: 12, 11, and 9 feet. Yet, in the next sentence, the contract tells us that "the steares, conveyances & divisions without & within" should be executed exactly the same as in the Globe. I think we may conclude from this that the shape and dimensions of the Fortune differed from those of the Globe, that the Globe was not a square and that its galleries had different proportions. More than that we do not know.

Dimensions are also given for the stage of the Fortune. The width is set at 43 feet, and in depth the stage is "to extende to the middle of the yarde." Since the sides of square yard measured 55 feet, the stage must have been 27½ feet deep. No indication is given of the height of the stage platform, but the space under the stage was to be "paled in" with strong oak boards. Since the dimensions of the Fortune's stage was expressly mentioned in the contract, those of the Globe presumably differed, and I do not believe one is justified in transferring the dimensions of the Fortune's stage to that of the Globe, as J. C. Adams (1) has done. We know the dimensions of *one* Elizabethan stage, that of the Fortune Theatre, but this tells us nothing about the dimensions of the others. The dimensions which Adams "computed" for the Globe stage (43 feet × 29 feet) are thus purely hypothetical. On the other hand, Hodges' assumption that the space below the stage of the Globe Theatre was not covered is substantiated by the Fortune contract, which, after speaking of the covering, says, "And the saide Stadge to be in all other proporcions contryved and fashioned like vnto the Stadge of the saide Plaie howse called the Globe." Henslowe and Alleyn furnished the builder with a sketch ("plott"), which unhappily has been lost.

We also learn that the stage of the Fortune was provided with a roof ("shadowe or cover"). A roof of this sort is shown in the sketch of the Swan, and it may be assumed that the stage of the Globe was also covered. In the Swan the front of the roof was supported by two posts, but the Fortune contract makes no mention of any upright supports. Of this we shall have more to say later. In 1613, when Alleyn and Henslowe commissioned a builder for the Hope Theatre, they stipulated in the contract that the "Heavens all over the saide stage" should be "borne or carryed without any postes or supporters to be fixed or sett vppon the saide stage . . ." Since the Hope Theatre was also intended for bearbaiting, the stage had

14

to be removable; the whole yard was required for the bears and their tormentors. The space beneath the stage of the Globe could not have been left open because of the necessity of hiding substage operations, and Hodges believes that it was hidden by draperies, black ones for tragedy, etc. The Fortune contract stipulates that "all the princypall and maine postes of the saide fframe and Stadge forwarde" should be "square and wroughte palasterwise," topped with "carved proporcions called Satiers." It thus seems reasonable to assume that the corresponding ornaments in the Globe were round or semicircular. The "Scantlinges of the timber" employed by Streete at the Fortune Theatre were—according to the contract—to be larger than those he had used for the Globe.

This analysis of the Fortune contract sheds light on the structure of the Globe only in minor points: covering of the space below the stage, ornaments, size of the scantlings. There is no justification for transposing the dimensions of the Fortune Theatre to the Globe.

One final passage in the Fortune contract deserves note: "A Stadge and Tyreinge howse to be made erected & settupp within the saide fframe." These words were long ignored until a few years ago Hodges noted their importance. They contain the germ of a theory of the origin of the Elizabethan playhouse, which Hodges (22) developed. An older theory traced the Elizabethan form of theatre back to the stages that actors set up in inn yards in London and the provinces. These yards were not roofed over. Along their walls ran balconies from which one could

15

enter the rooms of the inn. The stage was set up in the yard. Behind the platform, curtains were let down from one of the balconies. These provided a space where the actors could change their costumes and await their cues. Exits and entrances were effected through slits in the curtains, and the gallery could be used as an upper stage. According to this older theory, when James Burbage was pondering the design of his projected Theatre, he thought of these inn yards and took over their gallery arrangement.

Hodges rejected this theory, arguing that the Elizabethan playhouse could not have been derived from the rectangular inn yards, but must have originated in the round arenas, also equipped with galleries, that had been used for the cruel sport of bear-baiting since the middle of the sixteenth century. He pointed out that if stage and dressing room were to be built inside the "fframe" formed by the galleries (as the passage in the Fortune contract stipulates), they must have been an independent unit, not merely an outgrowth of the galleries. What, then, was the origin of the platform with the dressing room behind it? Hodges called attention to the street theatres formed with trestle stages, which troupes of strolling players erected in the market places. The scaffolding supported a platform at the rear of which there was a curtained dressing room, a booth, forerunner of the tiring house. As the pictorial material assembled by Hodges shows, these market stages were built quite high; the old engravings show that the actors' feet were approximately on a level with the heads of the audience. Sometimes the space below the stage was covered with cloths, but often the supporting framework was left open to view. (In the Swan drawing the supports are visible precisely because the picture does *not* represent a performance; at performances they were probably covered.)

When James Burbage erected the first permanent theatre in the north of London, he put the stage supported by scaffolding (with dressing room) into the ring of the bearbaiting arena; and in 1600, when the Fortune contract was drawn up, the notion of an auditorium "frame" for the stage and tiring house was still alive. When Shakespeare (in the Prologue of *Henry V*) refers to his stage as "unworthy scaffolds," we are reminded of the humble origin of the platform stage. If the Elizabethan stage developed from the street theatres, we may also assume with Hodges that the platforms of the Theatre, the Globe, or the Fortune were elevated $5\frac{1}{2}$ to 6 feet over the floor of the yard. A high stage (Platter's "raised platform") offered a decided advantage: there was adequate room under it for the men operating the traps, and the "cellarage" would provide storage space for the larger properties that might have to emerge from below. Adams, who estimated the elevation of the Globe stage at only four feet, was forced to conclude that the earth below it was excavated. In the swampy ground of the Bankside such excavations must soon have run into water.

I have now cited all the important documentary evidence; it has contributed hardly anything to a reconstruction of the Globe Theatre. Not without curiosity, therefore, we turn to such books as Adams'

17

The Globe Playhouse and Hodges' *The Globe Restored,* only to find that they do not fulfill the promise of their titles. True, at first sight Adams would seem to have actually reconstructed the Globe in the course of his four hundred pages. But on closer scrutiny we find an unproved edifice resting on unprovable foundations. Hodges' book contains an abundance of stimulating ideas and valuable illustrations, but its author also has failed to "restore" the Globe.

I do not aspire to reconstruct the stage of the Globe Playhouse. The undertaking strikes me as hopeless. The available documents simply do not enable us to answer questions such as the following: How large was the acting area? Were the stage doors parallel to the front edge of the stage or at an oblique angle to it? What was the nature of the upper stage? What was the height of the tiring house? I am not certain we could answer these questions even if we had the Globe contract; the Fortune contract provides an answer only to the first of them. And it is very likely that in many matters the Globe contract instructed Peter Streete to proceed "according to the manner and fashion" of the Theatre.

But why all this emphasis on the Globe? Most of the thirty-six plays contained in the Shakespeare First Folio were not first performed at the Globe. Shakespeare had written and produced eighteen plays before he and his associates moved to the Globe. More than twenty plays had their openings on other stages, at the Theatre, the Curtain, at Court, at the Blackfriars. The plays were also performed "on the road," in provincial towns where the strolling players (and Shakespeare was one of them) had to content themselves with halls and yards that certainly bore no resemblance to the permanent theatres in London. (We know almost nothing of these tours, and yet when the plague was raging in London the players would absent themselves from the capital for months at a time.) We shall give special attention to the Court performances and to the Blackfriars. In general, however, our aim will be to reconstruct not the Globe Playhouse but a "Shakespearean stage." In pursuing this task we shall bear in mind the medieval legacy of the English theatre; by way of avoiding Adams' syncretism, we shall follow as closely as possible the stage directions in the quartos and the First Folio of Shakespeare's plays; and we shall again consult Thomas Platter and pay attention to Henslowe's inventory. In short, we shall work only with Elizabethan elements, in the hope that this method will lead us to a relatively pure picture of the Elizabethan stage, the "ideal type" of an Elizabethan theatre.

3. Sixteenth-Century Stage Forms

THE SIXTEENTH CENTURY is characterized by an extraordinary wealth of stage forms, which I have described elsewhere (32, 34). Some of these stages were decidedly medieval, polyscenic—that is, with mansions or *loca* in juxtaposition. Others had a definite Renaissance character, stressing the unity of place within a monoscenic setting. Still others incorporated stylistically heterogeneous elements, and we might call them hybrid forms. Certain stages strove for illusion while others can be defined as nonillusionistic or symbolic. Some had a static quality, others embraced the new dynamic principle of successive monoscenic localization.

When Burbage built his Theatre, Scriptural plays were still being performed on wagon stages. While the preparations for the *Osterspiel* of 1583 were in process in Lucerne, the Teatro Olimpico was being built in Vicenza. The Lucerne stage was purely medieval, a polyscenic stage of juxtaposition with decorative elements intended to be partly realistic and partly symbolic. Palladio's stage, on the other hand, was a monoscenic stage of illusion, static in quality, a pure product of the Renaissance. By 1545 Serlio had built and described a pure Renaissance stage, monoscenic (within the dramatic category), illusionistic, and static. The Badius Stage (in the woodcuts of the Lyons *Terence*, 1493) was also a pure Renaissance stage, monoscenic and static, though nonillusionistic. What was still static in Serlio became dynamic and

20

successive in the Florentine Intermezzi of 1585–86 and 1589, for which Bernardo Buontalenti created the monoscenic, illusionistic stage of succession. With this dynamically changeable, illusionistic stage we are entering the baroque period.

So far I have mentioned only stages representing pure types. But the sixteenth century also had its hybrid forms. The stage built for the *Laurentius Play* in Cologne (1581) was such a hybrid: a polyscenic stage of juxtaposition with partly symbolic and partly realistic elements. In this respect it was still quite medieval; but it had numerous Renaissance features, including the back cloth, the slits for doors, and a unity of place. In the same year the *Ballet Comique* was presented at the Palais Petit-Bourbon in Paris, and this court ballet was also a strange hybrid form. On the dance floor, to the right of the King, was a little forest décor with the shepherd god Pan, a medieval mansion despite the Arcadian turn. To the left of the King a cloud pavilion concealed the musicians from the audience. In the course of the performance wagon stages were pushed into the hall, at the lower end of which, across from the King's seat, a gently sloping, monoscenic, illusionistic stage in Renaissance taste was situated. In the foreground was the garden of Circe, with imitation fruit-laden trees and flower beds; farther back were two three-dimensional, battlemented towers and the walls of the castle of the enchantress who sat in the doorway; in the background was a curtain showing the contours of a city and landscape, painted in perspective by Jacques Patin. For a while Circe's realm was half-concealed by a diaphanous curtain, which was later lowered in the Roman manner. Styles were mixed grotesquely: in the foreground, the grove of Pan and the wagon stages; in the background, an illusionistic stage worked out in detail. With all its medieval character the Valenciennes stage (1547) reveals Renaissance influences, at least in the synthetic view of Hubert Cailleau, though it must be admitted that this miniature presents the scenic elements in a combination never used in the Passion Cycle. There is a wall at the back of the stage, and entrances and exits were made through doors in this wall. This brings a Renaissance element into what, with its juxtaposed *loca*, is otherwise a thoroughly polyscenic stage.

And now we come to another form of sixteenth-century stage, that employed by the players of England, the "Shakespearean stage." How shall we define its style? Was it symbolic or illusionistic, monoscenic or polyscenic, static or dynamic, medieval or Renaissance, pure or hybrid? These are questions that must be answered unless we wish to admit that we know nothing about Shakespeare's stage. In the following we shall seek information—necessarily by detours, because we lack the sketch that James Burbage presumably made before starting to build the Theatre. Little would be known of Valenciennes without Cailleau's miniatures, of the *Osterspiel* production without Cysat's ground plan, or of the *Ballet Comique* without the etching on the frontispiece and the description of the fete. We have only one contemporary picture of a public Elizabethan theatre: De Witt's sketch of the Swan. We must refer to it again and again, particularly since Shakespeare probably performed there at one time.

4. The "Shakespearean Stage"

(a) The Platform and the Traps

WE CAN safely assume that Shakespeare's plays were performed on a platform stage. The sketch of the Swan shows a platform; the contracts for the Fortune and the Hope both speak of a raised stage. The platform jutted far into the yard, and the audience stood around it on three sides. The repertories of all the troupes included plays calling for traps. Shakespeare himself, however, made little use of them. No doubt the infernal spirits in *Henry VI* emerged through a trap. The witches' cauldron in *Macbeth* rose up from below the stage and sank down again ("Why sinks that cauldron?"). Shakespeare's ghosts are in general the spirits of murdered men, apparitions which made their entrance quietly, without sulfur fumes, hence probably not through trap doors. Yet, presumably, every Elizabethan theatre had a large trap door in the middle of the stage. In some cases the opening must have been of considerable size, for there were playwrights who expected "a chariot with four devils harnessed to its pole" or several persons at once to emerge through a trap door. Some stages had additional smaller trap doors, whose location cannot be definitely established, though they were probably in the corners. (Adams assumed the existence of four such small traps at the Globe.) In my opinion, three were used at the beginning of the fourth act of Macbeth, first produced at the Globe.

Each witch entered through a small trap, while the cauldron was raised through the large one. After their dance, the three Weird Sisters vanished again through their traps. But this is pure conjecture. The Folio says only: "Thunder. Enter the three Witches." In any case, the large trap could probably fulfill its function only if it were operated by machinery. The small ones required no special apparatus: persons who appeared through traps simply climbed up a few steps to the stage. The "spawn of hell" always appeared surrounded by fire and smoke. Fireworks of this sort had kept audiences breathless in the Middle Ages, and there is no reason to suppose that the art of pyrotechnics had declined in Elizabethan London. Sometimes a trap (probably the large one) was used for fishing objects from the depths, as in *Pericles*, II. i, where a rusty suit of armor is pulled out of the sea, or in *Hamlet*, v. i, where the First Clown tosses skulls up out of the grave.

It is doubtful whether the stages of the Theatre, the Curtain, or the Globe had two lofty posts like those supporting the stage roof in the Swan sketch. Such posts took up precious space and barred the view of several spectators, though of course their massive appearance in the Utrecht document may be attributed in part to poor draftsmanship. The Fortune contract mentions no stage posts, though it does call for a "shadow." In any case, the Hope Playhouse had no vertical roof supports, for the contractor was requested to "builde the Heavens all over the saide stage to be borne or carryed without any postes or supporters to be fixed or sett vppon the saide stage." The specification was necessary in this case, because in other respects the Hope was a copy of the Swan, which did have roof supports. Therefore, it is unreasonable to assume that the Fortune had such supports simply because the contract does not expressly preclude them. The Fortune was built on the model of the Globe, just as the Hope was built on the model of the Swan. It is more logical to conclude that neither the Fortune nor the Globe had roof supports. The Swan was perhaps the exception.

Now we turn to the doors through which the actors made their entrances and exits. De Witt's sketch shows two such doors in the tiring house. In referring to the Shakespearean stage, we must consult the dramatist's stage directions, most of which handle entrances and exits by a simple "enter" or "exeunt." Even persons lying in bed "enter." In the case of simultaneous entrances from opposite sides, Shakespeare's stage directions mention the doors. In *3 Henry VI*, II. v, we read: "Enter a Sonne that hath kill'd his Father, at one doore: and a Father that hath kill'd his Sonne at another doore." In *Richard III*, III. i: "Enter one Citizen at one doore, and another at the other." In *Coriolanus*, I. ix: "Enter at one Doore Cominius, with the Romanes: At another Doore Martius." The same technique applies to forest scenes when persons appear from different directions. *A Midsummer Night's Dream*, II. i, provides an example: "Enter a Fairie at one door, and Robin Goodfellow at another." Thus we see that Shakespeare counted on two doors, and we may assume that, first in the Theatre and later in the Globe, there were two such doors leading from the tiring house to the stage. But Shakespeare required addi-

25

tional possibilities of entrances and exits, and this brings us to the questions of the "inner stage" and the "upper stage."

(b) *Pavilion or Alcove?*

Adams is the most recent among a long series of specialists who have supposed that there was a curtained alcove at the rear of the Globe stage. Adams called this recessed section in the tiring house "the study." He computed its dimensions to be 23 feet in width and 7 to 8 feet in depth. This theory of an inner stage has aroused justified opposition. The sketch of the Swan shows none, and Hodges has pointed out that the term "inner stage" is found in no contemporary stage direction. He therefore inclines, particularly in tracing the development from the market stage, to the hypothesis of a pavilion (booth) rather than an alcove. Note, however, that this pavilion had a function different from that of the booth on the market stages, where the players changed their clothes and waited for their cues. In the Elizabethan theatre the booth served as an auxiliary stage, a potential scene of action, separated by curtains from the rest of the stage. The auxiliary stage was commonly used when the stage directions called for a "discovery." Marlowe's Doctor Faustus was thus "discovered" in his study (perhaps even in a medieval, mansion-type cell), as were the lovers playing chess in *The Tempest*.

Ludwig Tieck (42) arrived at very much the same idea, the pavilion, in the 1830's—intuitively as it were, for he lacked even the few documents that have come to light since. In his short story *Der junge*

Tischlermeister (written 1836), he attempted a reconstruction of Shakespeare's stage. Tieck's guiding principle was to "move the players up front, as close as possible to the audience"—undoubtedly a genuinely Elizabethan principle that was forgotten by his successors. In the center of a platform stage Tieck set two pillars "ten feet in height, supporting a rather broad balcony [*Altan*]" that was placed against the background of a hall. Under the balcony and between the columns was a "small inner stage," raised three steps high, which was sometimes open and sometimes concealed by curtains. "Rather broad steps led up to the balcony on the right and left." (The location of these stairs cannot be proved; they should be relegated to the tiring house.) Here again Tieck recognized the correct principle, as might be expected from one who disapproved of the proscenium-frame stage. He saw the advantages of his arrangement for the formal grouping of the actors:

> On these [stairs leading to the balcony] sat the councils and parliaments, and with a few persons the stage seemed filled, because the space to right and left was limited . . . The dying fell on the steps [leading to the pavilion] and of course lay there much more picturesquely than in our theatres; melancholy or contemplative characters leaned against the pillars; Macbeth, or Falstaff in *The Merry Wives of Windsor* mounted the steps to the right or left; on the upper balcony stood the burghers, parleying with King John and King Philip; down below,

27

raised on the stairs, sat the King and Queen in *Hamlet;* here was Macbeth's banquet at which Banquo appeared. The advantage of this arrangement is evident without any long-winded lecture. Two clearly distinct groups could stand on the right and left of the proscenium; if one hung back a little, the fiction that the other did not notice it seemed quite natural; in the case of two individuals it appeared still more natural. A third group stood or sat higher up, on the smaller inner stage which, thanks to this arrangement, was close to the spectators. One character never concealed another. . .

Compared with this, Adams' reconstruction is a regression, for his inner stage removes a part of the action from the audience. Hence, it is no accident that Adams called his alcove the ancestor of the picture-frame stage. It is conceivable that in the years between Shakespeare's death and the closing of the theatres in 1642 the inner stage underwent such a development. But we still know too little about stage design in the period of James I and Charles I to be certain, and there is no reason to suppose that this development had begun before Shakespeare's retirement from the stage.

Though Tieck may have been mistaken in minor details, he had a sound general view of the Elizabethan stage when he wrote, "This older theatre . . . itself participates in every scene; it may even be regarded as one of the main characters; it makes things easier for the actor, helps him, sustains him; he does not stand forsaken in an empty, deserted rectangle, but always has something to lean on mentally and physically." The spectators were drawn into the play and not treated like outsiders spying through a keyhole: "The drastic separation of our stage from the audience is utterly inartistic and barbaric; even before, but particularly after the curtain rises, the house looks as if one-half of it had broken off. We do our best to frustrate any communication between stage and audience."

We return now to the subjects which prompted this digression: Adams' alcove, which we reject on aesthetic grounds, and the pavilion.

Adams is convinced that there was a trap door in his alcove. Certain scenes, that any skillful showman would project forward, could thereby be moved as far away from the audience as possible: the gravedigger scene in *Hamlet*, for example, or the witches' scene in *Macbeth*. When we read in a modern edition the stage direction for *Macbeth*, iv. i, we must bear in mind that "A dark cave" or "A Cavern" was not Shakespeare's doing; this designation of locale was added by an eighteenth-century editor. The same is true of other localizations, which were inferred from the dialogue and added not only to help the reader but also to meet the production requirements of the only stage known in the eighteenth century, the painted picture-frame stage. Only the notion of a "dark cave" could lead a commentator to place the scene in an alcove. We prefer Tieck's advice, which would move the witches' scene close to the audience, with the cauldron on the big trap and the witches on three smaller traps. The scene is not only impressive but also Elizabethan if acted in the middle of the stage. In line 106 Macbeth asks, "Why sinks that cauldron?" We may definitely assume that at that moment the witches' cauldron sank below the stage, although we cannot support Adams' notion that the cauldron descended so that the spectators might have a better view of the ghostly royal procession. Adams has the eight kings "walk in single file through the passageway behind the study." This is hardly credible. Rather, we imagine the march of the kings in the forefront, with the single file of spirits entering through one door and leaving through the other. The spectators could then see the details which they were entitled to see: the magic mirror, the "two-fold balls," the "treble sceptres," the "blood-boltered" Banquo. The stage direction calls for "A *show* of eight Kings." Shakespeare was surely too much of a showman to let his kings parade in the dark background of an alcove.

When we look around for an Elizabethan witness to the pavilion, we find unexpected support for Tieck's contention in Thomas Platter's report of the performance at the Curtain Theatre. At one point in the unnamed play, the German warrior and his servant fall into a drunken sleep, and of this scene Platter writes, "Meanwhile the Englishman climbed into the tent [*in die Zelten*]" and abducted the girl. Since we are dealing with a battle scene, we might take the word "tent" in a literal sense and suppose that a soldier's tent had been pitched on the stage. But I prefer to follow Hotson (26), who assumes that Platter employed "tent" here to mean a pavilion-like booth. Another Alemannic writer, the Alsatian Martin Montanus, also used the word *Zelt*, meaning mansion, in his stage directions for *Von zweien Römern*, which appeared some time after 1560. Such a tent is described in the stage directions for Johannes Heros' tragedy *Der irrdisch Pilgerer* (1562) : "First, on the square where the play is to be given, a tent [*zellt*] should be put up and hung with tapestries [*teppichen*] round about; behind the tapestry a fully made bed." Thus Platter's tent is Tieck's and Hodges' pavilion. In the performance which Platter witnessed, the tent represented an inner room, while the platform no doubt represented the scene of the preceding battles over the girl.

Tents in the literal sense were also employed on the Elizabethan stage. In *Richard III*, v. iii, two tents were required at the same time, one for the King, the other for Richmond. Here again Adams squeezes the scene into his narrow alcove, allotting one half of it to Richard, the other to Richmond. This suggests a lack of feeling for the theatre and a poor understanding of the spirit of the times. When Richard entered with the words "Here pitch our tent" and a few lines later commanded, "Up with my tent," every Elizabethan expected a real tent to be pitched. Richard, accompanied by the officers of his staff, then went out through the same door by which he had entered. Through the opposite stage door entered Richmond with his staff. Anticipating his order, his soldiers (stagehands in disguise) began to set up a tent for their general—on the platform, of course, on the other side of which Richard's tent was already standing. In reading the ensuing scene, one has the feeling that it would be more effective if both Richard's and Richmond's tent remained open:

31

the peacefully slumbering Richmond and Richard haunted by ghosts create an effective contrast, which Shakespeare as a showman would not have missed. In any case, the scene is wholly in the spirit of the Middle Ages: the tents, only a few feet from each other, are simply "mansions," in which almost simultaneous actions take place. Adams, as we have said, places this scene in the alcove of his reconstructed Globe. It might be mentioned in passing that we have no proof that *Richard III* was ever produced at the Globe. It is one of Shakespeare's early plays, written perhaps as early as 1594 and consequently intended for Burbage's Theatre. It was certainly in the repertory of the Chamberlain's Men in the summer of 1597, when they were compelled to play in the provinces for several months. There they found no alcove and surely expected none, for in the Theatre as on the road they used in *Richard III* real tents that were set up on the platform. And, of course, they also carried Platter's "tent," the pavilion which they could place against any background.

(c) Décor—Spoken or Real?

One of the many widespread myths about the Elizabethan theatre is that the dramatists of the time made up for the lack of illusionistic elements by more or less poetic descriptions from the mouths of their characters. Poetry, by this theory, becomes a substitute for scenery. Its proponents point to the Chorus' speeches in *Henry V*, who apologizes at the beginning of each act because certain things cannot be shown on the stage but are left to the imagination of the spectator;

                              can this cockpit hold
The vasty fields of France? Or may we cram
Within this wooden O the very casques
That did affright the air at Agincourt?
O, pardon! since a crooked figure may
Attest in little place a million;
And let us, ciphers to this great accompt,
On your imaginary forces work.

And four lines further on:

Piece out our imperfections with your thoughts;
Into a thousand parts divide one man,
And make imaginary puissance;
Think, when we talk of horses, that you see them
Printing their proud hoofs i' th' receiving earth . . .

Repeatedly the Chorus appeals to the spectator's imagination: "Suppose that you have seen"—"O, do but think"—"Follow, follow!"—"Work, work your thoughts!" But what he is saying in these apologies is that a cavalry regiment cannot be shown thundering across the stage, that the arrival of the fleet in France must be left to the imagination of the audience, that only a slice of the siege of Harfleur can be shown, that time must be compressed. The Chorus merely reminds the audience of the fictions of the theatre; he does not say that the stage will remain bare and that no scenery will be used. Actually, the original stage directions and the texts of Elizabethan plays refer repeatedly to the presence of both flat set pieces and three-dimensionally constructed pieces. It is with these pieces of décor that we must now concern ourselves.

What do the documents indicate? In the sketch of the Swan we see only a bench. If I am right in assuming that De Witt's sketch shows the theatre during a rehearsal, the bench might be simply a rehearsal accessory, which in the actual performance was exchanged for a seat within a larger set piece. Let us take a concrete case. I can imagine that in a rehearsal of Kyd's *Spanish Tragedy* the love scene (ii. iv) was played with a bench only, as in the sketch of the Swan, but that in the actual performance the bench was placed in a "bower," to which Horatio and Belimperia withdrew. It is a night scene, and since the Elizabethan public stage knew darkness only by description, the poet's verses had to provide the atmosphere, which indeed, thanks to Kyd's poetic genius, unfolds in a spoken music that reminds one of *Tristan*. But the bower must have been real, for after the interrupted love scene Horatio is hanged in it and in it his dangling corpse is found by his father. I am convinced that in the performances of *The Spanish Tragedy* a medieval "house," a bower-like mansion, was on the stage and that it looked much like the bower represented in the woodcut in the 1615 quarto.

Moreover, there are contemporary proofs of the existence of such medieval elements on the Elizabethan stage. On March 10, 1598, Philip Henslowe, owner of the Rose Theatre, drew up an inventory (15) which enumerates the set pieces and properties the Rose possessed at a time when Shakespeare had already written over a dozen plays, and when he and his associates were planning to build a new theatre on the southern bank of the Thames. The items in Henslowe's stock included a rock, three tombs, a "Hell mouth" (perhaps for the final scene of Marlowe's *Doctor Faustus*, but at all events a thoroughly medieval article), a cage (apparently large enough to lodge Bajazeth in Marlowe's *Tambourlaine*), one "pair of stairs" for a play about Phaëton, two steeples, a beacon, "the sittie of Rome" (of which we shall have more to say below), a bay tree, a "tree of golden apples" (for the labors of Hercules), a "wooden canopy," a small altar, a bedstead, two "moss banks," a "Bellendon stable," and a "chain of dragons."

This invaluable document indicates that the Elizabethan stage—in this case, the Rose Playhouse in the year 1598—was by no means a desert, rather that certain actions were definitely pin-pointed by means of free-standing scenic elements. Anyone who supposes that when an Elizabethan actor was called upon to climb a tree he simply mounted one of the supports of the stage roof may begin to have his doubts when he reads that the Rose possessed several trees. True, neither the tree in the Garden of the Hesperides nor that of Tantalus was meant to be climbed, but a spectator could scarcely be expected to accept a stage post (if there were any in theatres other than the Swan) as a tree once he had seen authentic-looking trees in the Hercules and Tantalus scenes. When an Elizabethan actor stood on a rock, he stood on something that the spectator recognized as such. The same is true of the altar and of the steeples, which were painted to look like steeples and were probably three-dimensional. The character of the tombs in Henslowe's inventory remains a mystery: if they were designed for action inside a tomb, they must have had the height of sizable mansions; if they served as background for a mourning scene, they could be modest in size and not necessarily three-dimensional. They were probably sarcophagi, while Platter's tent-pavilion was used for tombs in which a scene occurred (e.g. *Romeo and Juliet*, v. iii). This subject will be discussed later.

Our attention is now drawn to the mysterious "sittie of Rome." W. W. Greg (15) was of the belief that it was used for *Doctor Faustus*. Was it a painted background, depicting the Castel Sant Angelo, the Tiber bridges, and perhaps St. Peter's? Such backgrounds were already in use in France, as noted in connection with the *Ballet Comique*. Or did it consist of a three-dimensional gate with bits of wall to the right and left (as in Circe's palace in the *Ballet Comique*) and an inscription identifying it as Rome? We can scarcely give a cogent answer to these questions, although the question will again arise in discussing the Court performances.

Henslowe's inventory also includes various celestial phenomena, such as a rainbow and a "clothe of the Sone and Mone." The nature of the cloth is mysterious, but it was certainly painted. If the "sittie of Rome" had been a curtain, Henslowe might have referred to it as a "clothe" and, since he did not, one may argue that "Rome" must have been a three-dimensional structure. But these matters cannot be settled by logic. In any event, the "cloth of the sun and moon" is again a medieval reminiscence; the book of expenditures for the Passion Play in Mons (1501) contains such an item: a *"piece ayant deduit le soleille et la lune."* This cloth was used for the story of the Creation.

Henslowe's inventory leaves no doubt that the stage of the Elizabethan theatre was equipped with ornaments. When Fynes Moryson (6) visited the Frankfurt Autumn Fair in 1592, he had occasion to attend a performance of English strolling players. The Englishman was ashamed of his compatriots:

> Germany hath some fewe wandring Comeydians, more deseruing pitty than prayse, for the serious parts are dully penned, and worse acted, and the mirth they make is ridiculous, and nothing lesse than witty . . . So as I remember that when some of our cast dispised stage players came out of England into Germany, and played at Franckford in the tyme of the Mart, hauing nether a complete number of Actours, nor any good Apparell, nor any ornament of the Stage, yet the Germans, not vnderstanding a worde they sayde, both men and women, flocked wonderfully to see theire gesture and Action, rather than heare them, speaking English which they vnderstoode not . . .

Moryson's reproach that these English players lacked stage decorations suggests that the actors would not have dared to appear in London without "ornament of the Stage." Here we have indirect proof of the use of properties, substantiating our conclusions from Henslowe's inventory.

5.   Court Performances with Mansions

BEFORE continuing our investigation of the public theatres, we must note briefly the Court performances, particularly because Shakespeare and his associates frequently played at Court.

The principal season for these performances encompassed the days following Christmas, from St. Stephen's to Epiphany. Occasionally plays were also given at Candlemas and during carnival time. Under Queen Elizabeth there was an average of six to ten such performances; in the season of 1600–01 there were eleven. Under James I the performances often began in November and continued with interruptions until past Easter. In the season of 1609–10 no less than twenty-three performances were given. Several halls were available for the purpose in Whitehall Palace, and each of the royal castles (Hampton Court, Greenwich, Richmond, Windsor) had at least one large hall where plays could be given.

Each autumn the leading London troupes were invited to submit a list of their plays to the Lord Chamberlain. From these lists the officials chose the plays that seemed to them best suited to the Court. Thus all the plays given at Court were picked from the repertories of the public theatres. They were first played before an official who examined them for passages that might give offense. At these trial showings it was also established what sets, costumes, and properties would be needed. For certain plays the entire décor had to be prepared at Court; this was the responsibility of the Office of the Works. Sometimes the players themselves were expected to provide a part of the necessary equipment in acceptable repair, and the Office merely filled in deficiencies. For an appearance at Court a troupe was paid an average of ten pounds.

The halls were arranged in the Florentine style. The Queen sat approximately in the middle on a canopied throne on a raised platform. Between the throne and the stage situated at the end of the hall there was an empty space. As in the Uffizi Theatre, the audience sat along the walls on "degrees" (*gradi*). In his reconstruction of the Court performance of *Twelfth Night* on January 6, 1601, Leslie Hotson (27) developed the theory that the stage at Whitehall Palace was surrounded by the audience on all four sides, in other words that Shakespeare produced "in the round." He based his theory on a passage in a letter written by Don Virginio Orsini, Duke of Bracciano, to his wife in Florence. The Duke informed his *consorte amatissima* that at this performance the ladies had sat on *gradi* which were disposed *atorno atorno*. Hotson took this repetition of *atorno* rather too literally, as meaning "on all four sides." I have proved (35) that it need not have had this meaning. For example, Bastiano de' Rossi, in his description of the *Amico fido* as staged by Bernardo Buontalenti at the Uffizi Theatre in 1585–86 relates that the ladies sat on *gradi* which surrounded the hall *intorno intorno*. We know that the *gradi* were not on all four sides: for Buontalenti's stage was situated on the fourth side. Thus the repetition of *atorno* or *intorno* meant nothing more than on three sides. And when in a memorandum of the Lord Chamberlain we find the words "degrees placed rownd about," we must not interpret this pedantically, in support of an untenable arena theory. In the large hall of the Uffizi, as at Whitehall, the stage was set up at one end of the hall, and the audience nevertheless sat "rownd about," namely along the unoccupied walls.

Preparations for the Court performances were entrusted to the Office of Revels, headed by a Master who was directly under the Lord Chamberlain. In a document dating from the fifteenth year of the Queen's reign (1572–73), the duties of this Master of the Queen's Revels were exactly defined: "The cheife busynes of the office resteth speciallye in three poyntes In makinge of garmentes In makinge of hedpeces and in payntinge. The connynge of the office resteth in skill of devise, in understandinge of historyes, in iudgement of comedies, tragedyes and shewes, in sight of perspective and architecture some smacke of geometrye and other things." His accounts were carefully kept. From these "Revels Accounts," published by Feuillerat (11) we learn that certain structural units, called "houses" in our source, were fashioned for the Court performances. A house of this sort consisted of a wooden frame on which painted canvas was stretched. The book of accounts includes the following items: "canvas to couer diuers townes & howsses," "howses of paynted canvas," "sparres to make frames for the players howses," "hoopes for tharbour & topp of an howse," "canvas to paynte for howses for the players & for other properties as monsters, greate hollow trees," and finally, "ffurre poles to make rayles for the bat-tlementes & to make the prison." It has been reck-oned that an average of sixteen square yards of can-vas was used for a house. For the performances of the season of 1567–8 the artisans provided the fol-lowing mansions: "Stratoes howse, Gobbyns howse, Orestioes howse, Rome, the Pallace of prosperitie Scotlande & a gret Castell one thothere side." The acquisitions for the season of 1579–80 are particu-larly instructive, because we know for what plays they served. For *The Four Sons of Fabius* "a Cytie, a Mounte" were built; for *Sarpedon*, "a greate Citie, a wood . . . A Castell"; for *Portio and Demoran-tes*, "A cytie a towne." In 1582–83 "one Cloth and one Battlement of Canvas" were required for a play at Windsor Castle. The following items are listed for a performance of *Phyllida and Corin* at Greenwich Castle, 1584–85: "one great curteyne . . . one mountayne and one great cloth of canvas." Numer-ous entries refer to three-dimensional trees: "A tree of Holly for the Duttons playe . . . other holly for theforest" (1572–73).

Rocks were often mentioned, including one that seems to have been rather complicated, used for *The Knight of the Burning Rock* (1578–79). First, three carpenters were paid for their work on the rock. A blacksmith then put in a bill for "A scalling Ladder that serued at the Rock"—presumably a hidden stairway enabling one to reach the top of the rock from behind. We know that the rock was painted from another bill "ffor Coales at the courte to drie the Painters worke on the Rock." "Ivy and holly for the Rock" were also noted. In the course of the play, as the title indicates, the rock had to take fire; this called for "Aquavite to burne in the same rock." A cloud was connected with the rock, for "blewe Lynnen cloth" was ordered to mend the cloud that had not been procured new but borrowed from the players. The cloud had to "serve the rock." "A coard & pullies" were purchased "to drawe vpp the clowde." This reminds one very much of the moveable clouds used in Bourges for the performance of the *Actes des Apôtres* in 1536, and the "aquavite" effect was also among the *secretz* of the mystery plays. Thus we shall not be surprised to encounter a medieval "monster" on the Elizabethan Court stage of 1572–73: it required seven ells of canvas—no doubt mounted on hoops, for we find the entry "hoopes for the monster." Inside the monster there was a man who made it move: someone received two and a half shillings "for playeng in the Monster."

In contrast to the little we know of the scenery used in the public theatres—Henslowe's inventory is our only source—we have, therefore, abundant material regarding the performances at Court; each year the players appeared at Court with a selection of their newest plays, and each year new "howses" and properties were fashioned for this purpose. Consequently, I cannot support E. K. Chambers (6) in his contention that these houses were intended merely as dressing rooms and had nothing to do with the performance of plays. If they had served *merely* as dressing rooms for the players, it would not have been necessary to build new mansions each year. Beyond a doubt, they were conceived as habitations for the dramatis personae, and the painters assuredly did

42

their best to supply the appropriate local color. As we have seen, a Master of the Revels was expected to possess a knowledge of history and an understanding of perspective. The "Pallace of prosperitie" was expected to look different from the "house of Orestes," and if real trees were brought in to make a forest look authentic, it is safe to assume that palaces, fortresses, and other structures were made recognizable by painting. It is not difficult to imagine what the mountain, the prison, or the bower may have looked like. It is harder to form an idea of the battlements, unless we suppose them to have been constructed to a man's height. The appearance of the "Cyties" remains a mystery. Was a city characterized by a gate and a label? Philip Sidney's protest against this medieval usage in his *Apologie for Poetrie*, ca. 1583, would support such an interpretation, for he writes: "What Childe is there that, comming to a Play, and seeing *Thebes* written in great letters vpon an olde doore, doth beleeue that it is *Thebes?*" Or should we think of a perspective painting on a "great cloth of canvas"? Is the "greate curteyne" of 1584–5 a painted backdrop of this kind, such as Jacques Patin prepared for the *Ballet Comique* in 1581?

But whatever these houses may have looked like, there can be no doubt that the stage employed in these Court plays was decidedly medieval: the different mansions, often representing localities far removed from one another, stood juxtaposed on the platform. Philip Sidney rejected this polyscenic type of stage on pseudo-Aristotelian grounds: "You shall haue Asia of the one side, and Affrick of the other, and so many vnder-kingdoms, that the Player, when he commeth in, must ever begin with telling where he is, or els the tale will not be conceiued." The Court stage cannot have been very different from the *Laurentius* stage in Cologne. There we find a mountain (Mons Caelius), a house for Faustina, a prison with bars, a throne with canopy, the gateway to the imperial palace, and such set pieces as an altar (an "Awlter for Theagenes" appears in the Court accounts for 1572–73, and Henslowe likewise possessed a "littell alter"), a statue, and a grating on which the saint was tortured (Henslowe owned a beheading machine). The platform of the Cologne stage was bounded on three sides by a yellow cloth. One cannot say definitely if this means that the "great cloth" or "curteyne" of the Court plays was a back cloth of this kind. It seems to me, however, that an examination of the *Laurentius* stage brings us closer to the English Court theatre. In any case, the *Laurentius* stage casts more light on the Elizabethan theatre than do the Badius woodcuts, the Serlian stage, or even the Rederykers.

Each year at Christmas time Shakespeare and his fellows acted on a stage of this kind. To my mind, these Court performances must have exerted a considerable influence on the public theatres. We should discard the notion of "bare boards." Undoubtedly, a good deal of medieval stage technique survived in the Elizabethan theatre, particularly in the years when the repertories consisted largely of romances about knights and sorcerers, which definitely called for the whole medieval apparatus. True, literary taste changed during the twenty years of Shakespeare's connection with the stage. The interest in romantic

44

tales of chivalry continued, but only among the lower classes, while the élite looked down on the uneducated apprentices who still took pleasure in such outworn themes. *The Knight of the Burning Rock*, still taken seriously in 1572–73 by a Court society, was burlesqued thirty years later in Beaumont's *Knight of the Burning Pestle* (1608).

Still, theatrical fashions are slower to change than literary ones, and it seems reasonable to suppose that not only in the Theatre and the Curtain but also in the Globe elements of the polyscenic theatre lived on. Economy and other practical considerations may indeed have led the troupes to limit the number of their houses; they may have attempted to get along with two doors, a few sets, and a pavilion that could be localized as required. But this sort of tent, which could represent a study in one scene and a tavern in the next, is itself a medieval device. I need only refer the reader to the list of "houses and courts" (*hüsse vnd höff*) that precedes the text of the Donaueschingen Passion Play (ca. 1485). In addition to the special mansions for Caiaphas and Herod, Pilate, and Annas, we find "a common castle [*gemeine burge*] in which to crown, scourge, perform the Last Supper and other things." In other words this "common castle" can change its identity. To my mind, the public Elizabethan theatre (in contrast to the Court theatre) possessed such a "common castle," and this area, which could be closed off by curtains—Platter's tent—came in the course of Shakespeare's lifetime to be relied upon more and more, while the number of the medieval scenic elements decreased.

Of course, this development cannot be reconstructed in detail; dating is out of the question, particularly since some of the theatres evolved more rapidly than others. For, then as now, there were both progressive and conservative theatres. I should reckon the Globe among the progressive theatres, while I should call the Red Bull, where Thomas Heywood's *The Golden Age* was produced in 1611, conservative, if not old-fashioned. The tent, related in function to the medieval common castle and essentially a neutral pavilion that could be localized at will, was assuredly the most important of the properties that the Elizabethan players took with them on their wanderings in England and on the Continent. They also carried a curtain to serve as a back cloth. Two slits in the curtain permitted entrances and exits on the right and left. In the center, the tent was placed against the curtain; an additional opening in the middle of the curtain made it possible to enter the pavilion from the rear. This provided three entrances. Apart from the pavilion, the company would carry the most necessary set pieces of the kind listed by Henslowe.

6. *The Upper Stage*

THUS FAR we have disregarded a fourth means of
entrance, the upper stage, which was sometimes employed in the Elizabethan theatre. When we encounter "above" or "aloft" in the stage directions,
we know that the author or director desired an entrance on a raised level. Not content with an alcove
on the main stage, Adams gives us another on the
upper level; this second alcove, according to him, lies
behind a balustrated balcony, or "tarras." It is thus
that he pictures the upper stage of the Globe Playhouse. He then proceeds to stage certain "interior
scenes," such as *Hamlet*, III. iv, and *Cymbeline*, II. ii,
on this upper level. No early edition puts either of
these scenes "above." In both scenes it is extremely
important that the spectator should see the details.
Adams' upper stage, situated behind a little terrace
protected by a balustrade, has an "arras" or back
cloth and "side hangings." Behind which curtain does
Polonius hide? Adams chooses the arras for a purely
theatrical reason: the ensuing identification of the
corpse "must be in full view of the audience." Adams'
imagination surpasses all bounds: how can a spectator standing down in the yard be expected to identify a body situated twelve feet up behind a curtain
eight feet back (or eleven feet if the balcony is taken
into consideration)? One can scarcely conceive of an
arrangement showing less feeling for the theatre. I
am convinced that the scene between Hamlet and his
mother, one of the most important in the play, was

enacted where all could see it, namely in our tent. It is pointless to argue that the preceding scene, in which Hamlet finds the King praying and does not kill him, is also an interior scene, and that two such scenes could not be played successively in the tent. Claudius doubtless prayed at some point on the platform, as far downstage as possible, facing the audience while Hamlet stood behind him. The stagehands probably brought in a praying stool, which they carried out again as the curtains of the tent opened for Polonius' entrance into the Queen's closet.

Cymbeline, II. ii, was also played in the tent and not on Adams' upper stage. Everything had to be visible to the audience: the trunk in which Iachimo is smuggled into Imogen's bedchamber and the villain's lascivious gestures as he regards the lovely, defenseless sleeper. This last could be effective only if the spectator saw the details. It is inconceivable that the scene was not played in the tent.

But what about scenes that the author distinctly situated "above"? In *Romeo and Juliet*, III. v, the Second Quarto has the stage direction "Enter Romeo and Juliet aloft," and the First Quarto has "Enter Romeo and Juliet at the window." I have no doubt that, if this play had been produced at the Swan, the scene would have been played on the gallery, though assuredly in front, close to the balustrade, as indicated by the many references in the *aubade* to the signs of approaching dawn. At the hurried entrance of the Nurse (Q1: "Enter nurse hastily"), Romeo lets himself down to the platform by a rope ladder (Q1: "He goeth downe"). It is probable that every public theatre had a gallery. It was on this gallery that Gloster appeared between two bishops (*Richard III*, III. vii), and Brabantio was roused from sleep by Iago (*Othello*, I. i).

Even though we assume that all the public theatres possessed galleries like the Swan's, we must also consider another possibility, namely that the roof of the tent was flat and solid (perhaps surrounded by a low balustrade), and that the players could reach it from the gallery to play the "above" scenes. This would have provided a suitable place for "above" scenes presenting important detail, as we shall see below in connection with the monument scene in *Antony and Cleopatra*. In any case, we are back again at Tieck's loggia and balcony. The tent with the flat, accessible roof also has a medieval prototype. Vigil Raber's sketch for the Palm Sunday play in the Parish Church at Bozen in 1514 shows, in the middle of the platform, a pavilion designated as the temple of Solomon. Its flat roof is inscribed *pinaculum*, suggesting that the temptation scene was played there.

By way of verification, let us refer back to our documents. Henslowe does not mention a tent. But he could not have produced the plays in the repertory of the Rose with the properties listed in the inventory. He needed the neutral tent. If he failed to mention it in the inventory, it is perhaps because the pavilion was just as essential a part of the stage as the platform itself, which is not mentioned either.

In view of De Witt's sketch we must now ask where this tent was set up at the Swan. The only possible place is the space between the two doors of the tiring house. The players had to have access to the tent from behind; they had to be able to enter it unobserved by the audience. The only logical solution is that the whole breath of the tiring house beneath the gallery was concealed by a curtain, a "great cloth." This curtain is not a product of my imagination. In his *Gull's Hornbook* (1609) Thomas Dekker advises his gallant, who wishes to witness a play from a seat on the stage, not to "enter" too early, but only after the trumpeter has given the signal for the play to begin. "Then it is time," says Dekker, "as though you were one of the Properties, or that you dropt out of the Hangings, to creepe from behind the Arras . . ." The hangings and arras here mentioned permit us to presume the existence of a back cloth from which the "fethered Estridge" would creep as though he were "one of the Properties." This curtain also covered both doors. The tent was placed against the middle of the curtain, which must have had three openings, probably slits, one in front of each door and one in the middle, this last being the rear entrance to the tent. If the Swan had had a middle door, the curtain would have been superfluous and the tent would simply have been moved up to that door. In all events, there is hardly an Elizabethan play for which two entrances would have sufficed. The absence of curtain and tent in De Witt's sketch is once again explained by the fact that the sketch represents a rehearsal—the actors were well aware that curtain and tent would be in their usual places at the actual performance. Today actors often rehearse against the backstage fire wall, in the justified assumption that at the opening, if not at the dress rehearsal, there will be a painted back-

Detail from the frontispiece to Roxana Tragaedia *(1632), a play attributed to William Alabaster. The curtain in front of the tiring house gave the players at least three possibilities for entrance and exit (left, right, and center), at any rate more than the two choices afforded by the Swan stage.*

Detail from the frontispiece to The Tragedy of Messalina *(1640), a play by Nathaniel Richards. Another view of such an upstage curtain, an absolutely essential piece of equipment for traveling companies.*

drop or cyclorama. A curtain of this kind is shown in two pictures of contemporary stages, though we can no longer identify the theatres: the vignettes on the title pages of *Roxana* (1632) and *Messallina* (1640). In both cases a curtain terminates the stage at the rear—no doubt the actors made their entrances and exits through openings in it.

7. *Shakespeare's Staging of* Romeo and Juliet

ALL THIS is hypothesis, but it is hypothesis built exclusively on elements of the Elizabethan theatre and, moreover, on elements whose medieval roots cannot be denied. We shall now attempt to describe the first performance of *Romeo and Juliet*, a tragedy written for the public theatre. We shall follow the Elizabethan stage directions implicitly, hoping with their help to put our hypothetical stage—which is perhaps not so hypothetical after all—into operation. Our sources will be the First and Second Quartos (1597, 1599). These early and, for the most part, unauthorized editions of Shakespeare's plays contain no indications of locale. Such locations as "The hall in Capulet's house" and "A street with shops," that we read in modern editions, have nothing to do with the Elizabethan stage. They were added by eighteenth-century editors for the convenience of the reader. But they very much impede the understanding of Shakespeare and his stage. The modern reader requires a "disintoxication cure": this he can obtain by reading Shakespeare in the Folio or in the various reprints of the Quartos. *Romeo and Juliet*, in particular, may be read in Richard Hosley's "Elizabethan" edition (24). This helps to dispel visions of the picture-frame stage created for unimaginative spectators, on which Shakespeare groans beneath the burden imposed on him by the scene painter, and the actors are hampered in their movements.

Romeo and Juliet was first performed in 1595, probably at Burbage's Theatre. The Swan was built in the same year. We have no authentic data concerning the Theatre, but we possess the sketch of the Swan. We are obliged, therefore, to keep the sketch in mind as we attempt to follow Shakespeare's directions, particularly since Shakespeare and his fellows very likely also played at the Swan. Let us then construct a "Shakespearean stage" on the basis of the material thus far examined. The two doors of the tiring house cannot be seen during the performance: they are covered by a curtain, which hangs from the gallery and has three openings. Before both doors there are slits in the curtain; the third opening is not visible, for in front of it stands the pavilion which extends up to the gallery. The tent itself is closed off with curtains. Tieck may even have been right in assuming that two or three steps led up to the tent.

In a play such as *Romeo and Juliet*, where the tragedy springs from the hostility between two families, it is important to separate the hostile camps in a purely visual sense. The Montagues—let this be our fiction—enter through the left door (or rather curtain slit), the Capulets through the right. Entrances through the tent will be referred to as entrances through the middle. The space surrounding the tent on three sides is the platform.

The Prologue, in traditional black mantle and bearing a laurel wreath, comes and goes through the middle. The play begins with the entrance of

Capulet's servants through the right door. They are met by the Montague servingmen coming from the left door. Benvolio, a kinsman of Montague, enters from the left; Tybalt, a kinsman of the Capulets, from the right. Then old Capulet and his wife appear from the right; old Montague and his wife, from the left. Prince Escalus enters from the tent middle and parts the opposing factions. The Montagues remain while the others go out through the doors by which they have entered. Romeo makes his first entrance from the left; Montague and his wife exeunt left. At the end of the scene, Romeo and Benvolio also go out on the Montague side. At this moment Capulet, Paris, and the Clown enter right, and Capulet and the Count exeunt right after giving the Clown the list of those invited to the banquet. Romeo and Benvolio enter from the left. The Clown returns to the Capulet house. Romeo and Benvolio exeunt left. Capulet's wife, the Nurse and, a few moments later (by way of preparing her entrance), Juliet enter through the right-hand door, by which they exeunt after the servant coming in from the right has informed them that all is in readiness to receive the guests. Enter Romeo, Mercutio, and "other Maskers" from the left. To the sound of music they enter, through the right door, the house of Capulet. Here Q2 has an interesting—and quite medieval—stage direction: "They march about the Stage"—to indicate their traveling a certain distance. While the Maskers disappear through the right door, the tent opens for the servingmen's scene in the Capulet house. The servingmen exeunt right, across the platform, and at the same moment Capulet with his guests enter middle into the tent, which for the first time is specified, here as the hall in Capulet's house. The scene begins in the tent but spreads over the platform: after a time, tent and platform together form the hall. Capulet's words "A hall, a hall! give room" were no doubt the cue for the expansion. The scene between Romeo and Juliet must have been played in an extreme downstage position. The director singles out the lovers just as the poet singled them out with the pilgrim sonnet (ll. 95–108). The guests go out center. The tent closes and is thus neutralized. The Nurse and Juliet remain for a while, then they leave through the Capulet door.

The Chorus appears, stepping out of the tent to speak the second prologue. He exits through the tent. Meanwhile, stagehands have placed two or three trees in front of the tent, trees such as we have seen in the Court performances and in Henslowe's inventory. This is Capulet's orchard. The stagehands also move out a section of wall, that is, a wooden frame covered with canvas, painted no doubt as the "battlements" were painted at Court. The wall extends from the left tent post to the front of the stage. Romeo comes in from the left and after speaking two lines leaps over the wall into the orchard. His friends also come in from the left and failing to see him go out again on the left. This does not mean that the wall must have been six feet high: Romeo no doubt "leaps" over a wall that he could easily have stepped over. The Japanese theatre still has such fictions, which are simply tacit agreements between the players and the public. Juliet appears on the gallery (though neither Q1 nor Q2 contains any such direction); Romeo is below, beneath the trees. The love scene follows. As soon as it is ended, the stagehands remove the trees and the wall (probably through the tent to the tiring house, by way of the center slit in the curtain), while Romeo exits left. At this moment Friar Lawrence comes out of the tent with a basket (Q2: "Enter Friar alone with a basket"), and later Romeo enters left. Both then exeunt center. Benvolio and Mercutio enter left. Romeo, coming in from center, joins them. Nurse and Peter come in from the right. The Montagues exeunt left, the Nurse and Peter right. Juliet delivers her soliloquy on the balcony. (Here the stage direction gives no help; it merely says "Enter Juliet"). The Nurse joins her. They leave the balcony in different directions, Juliet to seek out Friar Lawrence, the Nurse to procure the rope ladder. The tent opens, and in it we discover Friar Lawrence and Romeo. Later, they are joined by Juliet, who enters center. The Second Quarto has the stage direction "They embrace." The First Quarto: "Enter Juliet somewhat fast and embraceth Romeo." Here we probably have a reminder of one of the early performances: Juliet comes in quickly and later on (though again only in the First Quarto version) bids Friar Lawrence hurry: "Make hast, make hast, this lingring doth vs wrong." At the end of the scene the tent closes.

Mercutio and his friends enter from the left, Tybalt and his men from the right. Romeo comes in from the tent to stop the quarrel. Tybalt wounds Mercutio and flees to the Capulet house—that is, to the right. Benvolio supports the dying Mercutio, helping him out through the left door. Benvolio comes back through the same door and informs Romeo, who has not left the platform, that Mercutio is dead. Tybalt comes in from the right. Romeo and Tybalt fight, and Tybalt is killed. Romeo leaves center. Members of the hostile families stream in through their doors; the Prince may come in from either side. At the end of the scene (in which Romeo is banished) all return to their houses. Juliet, alone, appears on the balcony (again the stage direction says only: "Enter Juliet alone"). The Nurse comes in. The direction in Q1 is highly theatrical: "Enter Nurse wringing her hands, with the ladder of cordes in her lap." Juliet instructs the Nurse to take her ring to Romeo, who is hidden in Friar Lawrence's cell. The tent opens. The Friar calls the fearful Romeo to come in center. Later on, Romeo hesitates to hide in the Friar's "study." This is fortunate, for without his reluctance he would have run into the Nurse. A stage direction in Q1 preserves a feature of an early performance. In his despair Romeo wants to kill himself, as is evident from the text. Q1 has: "He offers to stab himselfe," but "Nurse snatches the dagger away." This detail can only have originated with the author-director. The scene is almost at an end, but the Nurse has not yet given Romeo the ring. A stage direction in Q1 makes it clear that the Nurse has started to leave when she remembers her mission: "Nurse offers to go in and turns again." Then she gives Romeo the ring and goes out center. The tent closes at the end of the scene. Old Capulet, his wife, and Paris enter right and exeunt, again right. Juliet and Romeo appear on the balcony.

This time Q2 says expressly: "Enter Romeo and Juliet aloft," and Q1 has "at the window." Later, Romeo lets himself down to the platform with the help of the rope ladder. When Juliet says "Then window, let day in and let life out," we must not suppose that a real window was used. After Romeo's exit Juliet must have come down (by way of the stairs backstage) to meet her mother. Q2 contains no reference to her descent. But in Q1 we find the stage direction "She goeth downe from the windowe." Because of the variants in the text of Q1 and Q2, we cannot be sure at which verse she descends. In any case, the scene between Juliet and her parents is played on the platform, having perhaps begun in the pavilion. But the pavilion must at the very latest have been closed when the parents go out, for it is used in the following scene with Friar Lawrence.

The Friar, Paris, and Juliet appear in the tent, and then it closes once more. A transitional scene is played on the platform, with entrances and exits on the right. Then the tent is opened, disclosing Juliet's bed (Henslowe's inventory included a "bedsteade"). Juliet delivers her soliloquy, takes her potion, and falls on the bed ("She falls upon her bed within the curtains," says Q1). The tent is closed. Preparations for the wedding with Paris proceed on the platform. The tent is reopened, probably by the Nurse, who tries to awaken Juliet. The following scene, with its numerous actors, probably begins in the tent and spreads over the platform. Then the members of the Capulet family (with the Friar and Paris) go out to the right. The Nurse remains on the stage with the musicians. Q1 has the direction: "They all but the Nurse goe foorth, casting Rosemary on her and shutting the Curtens." I take this to mean that the curtains of the tent are closed after the assemblage has cast rosemary on the corpse. In the end, Peter and the musicians also retire to the Capulet house.

Romeo is now in Mantua. He probably comes in through the left door, and possibly a stagehand has fastened a board inscribed "Mantua" over the entrance. Balthasar also comes in left. The apothecary's shop is probably the tent; if so, the apothecary emerges without opening it, for the tent is used immediately afterward for Friar Lawrence's cell. The tent opens for the scene with the two Franciscans, and then the curtain closes. Meanwhile, stagehands may have placed some yew trees on the platform. Paris and his page enter on the left "with flowers and sweete water," then Romeo and Balthasar return from the left. Meanwhile, Juliet's tomb is set up in the tent, which opens as Romeo speaks the words "Thus I enforce thy rotten jaws to open." The duel ensues. Romeo carries Paris' corpse into the tent, and takes the poison beside Juliet's bier. Friar Lawrence enters left and meets Balthasar waiting beside a yew tree. They enter the tent and find the dead Romeo. Juliet awakens and sends away the Friar, who goes out center. Q1 says "She stabs herselfe and falles." The watch and Paris' page enter right, the Friar and a watchman left, attendants left, the Capulets right, and Montague left. After the Prince's final words, the stage empties and the audience applauds. But at once the Clowns appear to sing and dance the merry jig, the Elizabethan version of a satyr play.

Our reconstruction of an Elizabethan performance gives an idea of the breath-taking pace at which one scene must have succeeded another. Opinions may vary concerning the details of my "prompt book." Absolute certainty is not to be expected any more than we can hope to establish an authentic text of *Romeo and Juliet*. For we still are in doubt as to what Shakespeare wrote. One may say that the Second Quarto is "good" and that the First Quarto is "bad." By that token II. v would be an unexciting scene, while the First Quarto provides a lively one. There are variants also for v. iii. In the First Quarto, Paris speaks seven moving lines while strewing flowers on Juliet's tomb; in the Second, he expresses his grief in conventional form, which has likewise found its admirers among the experts. What did Shakespeare actually have Paris say? There are many theories and they all sound very learned, but hopelessly hypothetical. In the last analysis, the most astute theory turns on personal taste. But even if we cannot determine which of the two versions is Shakespearean (and why might both of them not stem from Shakespeare; why should we deny him the right to revise?), we may be certain that both are Elizabethan. And this is about all the certainty we can hope for.

It is in this light that we have considered the problem of direction. We have worked solely with Elizabethan elements: we have taken the frame from the Swan; we have borrowed the tent from Platter, the properties from Henslowe, and the back cloth from the Court performances. Since the Swan had only two entrances (two doors), we have had to create a third. We do not know whether the Theatre or the Curtain had a third door in the center of the tiring house. It seems possible that the Globe contract provided for a middle door which would have made the back cloth superfluous: in this case the tent could simply have been placed up against the center door. At the Globe the tent may have been attached permanently to the back wall of the stage, so that the players could reach the roof of the tent from the gallery.

A rigid roof would, in any case, have solved the difficulties that modern scholars have invented in connection with the monument scene in *Antony and Cleopatra*, iv. xv. At the beginning of the scene, the Folio (our only source for the text) contains the stage direction "Enter Cleopatra, and her Maides aloft, with Charmian & Iras." "Aloft" leaves no doubt that Shakespeare meant the Egyptian queen and her attendants to appear in a raised place. Later, the dying Antony, whose men have carried him through one of the stage doors, is lifted up and laid down before Cleopatra, in whose arms he is to die. Once again Adams obscures our view of this wonderful scene by moving Antony's death into his upper, balustrated alcove. Dover Wilson (46) thinks that the monument was specially built for this scene, "a square painted wooden structure with a barred gate in front and a flat roof." At the end of the preceding scene the stagehands, he believes, have placed this structure over the central trap, whence

Cleopatra climbs a concealed stair to the flat roof. To complicate things still further, Dover Wilson also provides for a winch above the monument, with the help of which the dying hero is hoisted up.

All the objections that can be made to Wilson's "house" have been raised by M. R. Ridley (38) in the new Arden Edition of the play. Hodges favored a pavilion with flat roof, on which the Queen appeared (only in the first monument scene; in the second, v. ii, according to Hodges and Ridley, the whole platform was used). The dying Antony was lifted up to the flat roof by his men, with the help of Cleopatra's attendants. Hodges thus arrived at the conclusion to which these investigations have been pointing: the tent with Tieck's balcony. Hodges played with the idea that this pavilion was a permanent feature of the Elizabethan theatre. E. K. Chambers (6) had already spoken of a "porch-like projection from the back wall," as had Tieck a century earlier.

The monument scene may perhaps suggest the height of the roof platform. If it were seven to eight feet high, a few strong men could have lifted the body of the actor who played Antony (Burbage) to the flat roof. Then we can dispense with Wilson's cumbersome pulley hoist.

For the orchard and graveyard scenes in *Romeo and Juliet* we have assumed that trees were placed on the stage. Such three-dimensional trees were also used, no doubt, in *As You Like It*: Orlando needed a tree on which to fasten his love poem, and he speaks of other trees on which he means to carve Rosalind's name. Chambers once suggested that such trees appear through the trap. I regard this as unlikely; in all probability the traps were used only for magical effects. The bower for the play within the play in *Hamlet*, which Chambers has rising out of the trap, was carried in by stagehands, and the same is true of the bower in *Much Ado about Nothing*. But when a bower was conjured up by magic, it did spring out of the trap. This was the case in *A Looking Glass for London and England*, by Robert Greene and Thomas Lodge, where the ground is smitten with magic wands and a magnificent bower rises up out of the main trap.

Harley Granville-Barker (13), who was a scholar as well as a showman and never lost sight of the Elizabethan stage in his productions of Shakespeare, sometimes took a rather austere point of view. In his preface to *Romeo and Juliet*, for example, he says that the wall for II. i was to be supplied by the spectator's imagination. Goethe would have said, *"Das supponiere man!"* ("Let it be supposed"). The only stage direction in the Folio is "Enter Romeo alone" —there is no mention of a wall. Nevertheless, I have used a section of wall for the orchard scene. It is only a simple set piece compared with the walls that were used for *Henry VI*, *Henry V*, or *Coriolanus*. The battle scene at Corioli, for example, in the first act of *Coriolanus*, definitely required the use of a gate with pieces of wall on both sides. The preceding scene among the three women was presumably played in the tent. At the end of the scene, stagehands brought in the gate from the tiring house and placed it obliquely across the stage, roughly between one of the front tent posts and the nearest side edge of the

stage. The space between this gate and the stage
door behind it was Corioli. Coriolanus and his Romans entered through the opposite stage door and
commanded the trumpeter to blow alarums. There-
upon the two senators appeared on the wall of Corioli
and a little later, in the space set aside for Corioli,
the Volscians—who subsequently stormed out
through the gate and threw back the Romans. The
"exit" direction for Coriolanus is meaningless, as is
the subsequent direction to the effect that he re-
enters, cursing, for his speech makes it perfectly
clear that he is cursing. Here, the stage directions
of the Folio, our only source for this play, are
chaotic. The stage direction for i. iv. 42 tells us that
Coriolanus "is shut in" the city; in reality, he still
has three lines to speak. Then another stage direction says correctly, "Enter the Gati" (i.e. the gate),
and the gate is closed behind him. Evidently, he goes
on fighting in the Corioli area and vanishes, still fencing with the Volscians, into the tiring house. Outside
the gate his friends express their anxiety. Meanwhile, Coriolanus, pursued by the Volscians, emerges
from the tiring house and fights his way through to
the gate, which he opens, letting the Romans into
the city. Finally, all the contestants go out fighting through "Corioli." Thus we have an exciting
scene, thanks to the use of a set piece. It is not possible to determine at what point in the text the gate
was taken apart and carried away. It probably was
done during the sixth scene. In response to "let the
ports be guarded" in scene vii, it would only have
been necessary to post sentries before the stage door.

The capitol scene, ii. ii, in *Coriolanus* was probably played in the pavilion. In any case, chairs were set up in it, for the stage direction says, "Enter two Officers, to lay Cushions." The tent also served for the house of Aufidius in Act IV: the curtain opened for the servingmen's scene, and Aufidius entered from the background through the center door.

8. Backstage Operations

WE MUST now turn our attention to the upper stories of the tiring house. The musicians seem to have been located on the third floor. They were hidden from the audience, and the music presumably came out through a window. This window may occasionally have been used for dramatic purposes. In *1 Henry VI*, III. ii, the First Folio has the stage direction "Enter Pucell on the top, thrusting out a Torch burning." At the capture of Rouen, in other words, she no doubt waved her burning torch from the musicians' window. It is not certain whether the musicians' room was under or over the stage cover. At the Swan the musicians may have played behind one of the windows in the "hut," or loft, above the stage cover, and in this theatre Joan of Arc would probably have appeared with her torch at the spot where the trumpeter stands in the sketch.

The precious costumes were stored in the tiring house. The sound machines were situated in the attic. Here thunder was made (with drums or a "roul'd bullet" in a thunder-run). Here hung the alarm bells and the equipment for pyrotechnic effects. Here the "ordnances" or "peeces" went off. From the roof of the hut waved the flag which informed the people of London across the Thames that a performance was taking place this afternoon on the Bankside. And in the hut were blown the three trumpet blasts as a signal that the play should begin.

The man behind the stage responsible for the

smooth running of the performances is called "book-holder" in our sources (occasionally "book-keeper" or "prompter"). He combined the functions of stage manager and prompter. He "held" the "book" in the tiring house; but he was hidden from the public, unlike the medieval director-prompter, who held the *Dirigierrolle* before the eyes of the audience. The book-holder probably stood behind one of the stage doors or behind the curtains of the tent. One of his functions was to submit every new play to the Master of the Revels, a censor. We know the name of the book-holder of the King's Men in 1633: Edward Knight, who submitted the company's "books" to the censor, Sir Henry Herbert. Evidently Sir Henry had no desire to overwork. His directives to Knight show that he expected to receive an already expurgated text. After approving Fletcher's *The Tamer Tamed*, he wrote to Knight: "In many things you have saved mee labour; yet wher your judgment or penn fayld you, I have made boulde to use mine. Purge ther parts, as I have the booke." On another occasion Herbert warned the players not to learn their parts till he had "allowed of the booke."

A number of these books have come down to us. They were not mere prompt books, but also contained entries which on our present-day stage would be the concern of the stage manager. The book for Philip Massinger's *Believe as You List* contained notes relating to the properties that the players had to carry on entering: "Ent: Iaylor, with browne bread, & a woodden dishe of water." Other entries remind the stage manager that the stagehands must hold various properties in readiness for certain scenes. In Massinger's play, for example, a table with six chairs was needed for line 732. At line 654 the book-holder made the entry "Table ready: & 6 chaires to sett out." Several hundred lines before the actual cue the same prompt book contains the notation "All the swords ready." The trap would be needed only for line 1931, but at line 1825 the stage manager noted, "Gascoine: & Hubert below: ready to open the Trap doore for Mr. Taylor." Gascoine and Hubert were stagehands who were to assist the actor Joseph Taylor: they were sent below in plenty of time. Music and sound effects were also noted in the book. Occasionally, the stage manager noted the name of the actor rather than of the character in the book, and sometimes the actor's name made its way into the early printed editions. In the Second Quarto of *Romeo and Juliet*, iv. v. 102, we read, instead of "Enter Peter," "Enter Will Kemp," the actor who played the part of Peter. William Kempe's name also turns up in the Quarto (1600) of *Much Ado about Nothing:* it was he who played Dogberry. Perhaps Shakespeare himself, in writing the play, had the actor in mind, or it may have been the stage manager who first put in the actor's name. In any case, this quarto edition must have gone back to a theatre manuscript—we are not far from a Shakespearean prompt book.

Once the text was established (and occasionally sooner) the parts were distributed, and it was the duty of the book-holder to compare the parts with the wording of the prompt book. We recall Sir Henry Herbert's instruction to "purge the parts" in accordance with the book. For if this were not done something might remain in the parts that the Master of the Revels had deleted. Though we possess several original prompt books of the period, only a single Elizabethan part has come down to us (16). This is the title role in Robert Greene's *Orlando Furioso*, a play which enjoyed great popularity in the early 1590's, particularly since Orlando was played by the celebrated Edward Alleyn. This role, found in Alleyn's papers after his death, was originally an actual (medieval) "role," some seventeen feet long and six inches wide, consisting of pasted sheets of paper (now worm-eaten). It contains the text spoken by Alleyn (differing from the printed Quarto of 1594) and his cues.

The stage manager seems to have drawn up a synopsis of entrances and exits, i.e. a "plot," for each play. Six such manuscript plots have come down to us wholly or in part, and we have the wording of a seventh (16). They were pasted on cardboard and hung on a peg in the tiring house. The plot for the second part of the *Seven Deadly Sins* still reveals the square peghole. The first scene of the *Seven Deadly Sins* is described in the plot: "A tent being plast one the stage for Henry the sixt· he in it A sleepe to him The Leutenāt A purceuannt R Cowly Jo Duke and 1 wardere R Pallant· to them Pride· Gluttony Wrath and Couetousness at one dore· at an other dore Enuie Sloth and Lechery The Three put back the foure· and so Exeunt." Henry VI is a prisoner in the Tower; the Seven Deadly Sins appear to him in his sleep. A tent or pavilion was used for the Tower. To Henry come his warders, probably from the background of the tent. The Deadly Sins enter through the stage doors to the right and left. Here, in a document of the early 1590's, we have convincing evidence of the use of Platter's tent. Another plot, that of George Peele's *The Battle of Alcazar*, tells us that the Furies, before entering, are "Lying behind the Curtaines . . ." Certainly this is proof of the curtain discussed above, separating the whole breadth of the stage from the tiring house. The same play made use of "3 violls of blood & a sheeps gather," and the director noted these accessories in his plot. Here we have a memory of the bloodthirsty scenes that were as abundant in the Elizabethan theatre as in that of the late Middle Ages. Rather surprisingly, neither the plots nor the books indicate the doors by which entrances and exits were to be made. This must have been decided at rehearsals, for otherwise it is hard to see how confusion could have been avoided at performances; but here we are still groping in the dark. It seems likely that the stage manager of an Elizabethan theatre had an assistant who passed on his orders to the actors and stagehands.

9. Shakespeare's Actors

The company to which Shakespeare belonged
enjoyed the patronage of Lord Hunsdon, who was
appointed Lord Chamberlain in 1585. In the years
1590–93 the troupe dropped out of sight. In 1594
it seems to have revived and been joined by a number
of actors from Lord Strange's troupe. The rein-
forced Lord Chamberlain's troupe probably had its
headquarters at the Theatre. At any rate, Richard
Burbage, son of the Theatre's owner, soon developed
into the company's leading actor. In the last days of
December 1594 the Lord Chamberlain's Men played
at Court, and, as we mentioned earlier, Shakespeare
is first listed in the Court accounts, as an already
esteemed member of this company. We possess a list
of the actors belonging to the troupe in 1598, at
least those actors who took part in the first performance of Ben Jonson's *Every Man in His Hu-
mour*. Ten names were given: William Shakespeare,
Augustine Phillips, Henry Condell, William Sly, William Kempe, Richard Burbage, John Heminges,
Thomas Pope, Christopher Beeston, and John Duke.
Some of these actors will be discussed at greater
length below, but first let us follow the company's
destinies up to the time of Shakespeare's death.

In 1599 the Lord Chamberlain's Men moved to the
new Globe Theatre. Richard Burbage and his brother
Cuthbert had procured half the stock; five of the
actors shared the other half: Shakespeare, Pope,
Phillips, Heminges, and Kempe. After the Queen's

death in 1603, all existing troupes of players were placed under the patronage of various members of the royal family. James I took the Lord Chamberlain's Men into his service. Thus Shakespeare became one of the King's Men; as "groom of the chamber" he received an annual allotment of material for a livery to which he was entitled as a member of the royal household. In 1609 the King's Men opened a small roofed theatre, the Blackfriars, and Shakespeare became one of its "housekeepers," holding one-seventh of the shares. The troupe now played at the Blackfriars in the winter months, the Globe being essentially a summer enterprise. Toward 1610 Shakespeare seems to have retired as an actor. He spent the last years of his life in his native Stratford. On June 29, 1613, the Globe Theatre burned down. In June 1614 the second Globe Theatre, "the fairest that ever was in England" (according to John Chamberlain), opened its doors.

Thus Shakespeare wrote his plays for a troupe to which he himself belonged. He was thoroughly familiar with the personal talents and idiosyncracies of his fellows. Yet, unfortunately, casts for the original performances of Shakespeare's plays have not come down to us (as they have for those of Ben Jonson). In trying to discover who created the particular roles, we have nothing to go on but a few contemporary references; the rest is guesswork. On the basis of such allusions T. W. Baldwin (2) drew up an elaborate system of casts; this, however, was received with considerable skepticism.

Contemporary sources leave no doubt that it was Richard Burbage who first played Richard III,

Hamlet, Lear, and Othello. Baldwin assumes, and no one doubts, that Burbage also played the heroes and lovers in other Shakespearean plays. He played Prince Hal, Macbeth, Antony, Brutus, Pericles, Romeo, Bassanio, Claudio, Orlando, and Coriolanus; and if he played Lear, it seems reasonable to suppose that he also acted Prospero.

The comic character parts were played by Thomas Pope; he was Falstaff and Sir Toby Belch. Baldwin also gives him Shylock and, in general, all parts calling for swagger, e.g. Parolles and Armado. In 1603 such roles were taken over by John Lowin. The author of the anonymous *Historia Histrionica* (published 1699) recalls having seen Lowin as Falstaff (and as Morose, Volpone, and Mammon in Jonson's plays). Lowin is also believed to have created the role of Henry VIII. In any case John Downes tells us in his *Roscius Anglicanus,* published in 1708, that Thomas Betterton, who played this part at the time of the Restoration, had been instructed in it by Sir William Davenant and that Sir William "had it from Old Mr. Lowen," who in turn "had his Instructions from M. Shakespear himself." This is our only reference, and a late one at that, to Shakespeare's activity as a director. Lowin, it might be mentioned in passing, had started out as a goldsmith's apprentice and concluded his career as proprietor of the Three Pidgeons' Inn.

The foremost of the clowns in the troupe was William Kempe. Kempe had visited the Continent on several occasions before becoming one of the Chamberlain's Men. He passed as a master of the morris dance and displayed his art in the comic afterpieces, the

jigs with which every performance in the public theatres ended. His endurance as a dancer was amazing:
one day he made a bet that he could dance from London to Norwich, some 114 miles. This marathon
dance took thirty days. He is also described as
"dancing the morrice ouer the Alpes." Since he had
relatively small parts, he may have sought to at-
tract attention by improvisation. He left the Lord
Chamberlain's Men in 1599, and it has been thought
that Hamlet's attack on the improvisations of
clowns was directed against Kempe: "and let those
that play your clowns speak no more than is set down
for them, for there be of them that will themselves
laugh, to set on some quantity of barren spectators
to laugh too, though in the mean time some necessary question of the play be then to be considered.
That's villainous, and shows a most pitiful ambition
in the fool that uses it." In the First Quarto (1603)
the attacks are further amplified, and Hamlet quotes
some of the foolish quips bandied about by the clowns
"that keep one suit of jests, as a man is known by one
suit of apparel."

Kempe's successor was Robert Armin, who joined
the troupe in 1599 when it was playing at the Curtain. Armin created Touchstone, Feste, and the fools
in Shakespeare's mature tragedies: *Lear, Antony
and Cleopatra,* and *Timon;* he was perhaps the
porter in *Macbeth.* In Armin, Shakespeare seems to
have found a man of reliable intelligence. Perhaps
this would account for the appearance, from this
time on, of fools who are wiser than their masters.

John Heminges seems to have specialized in father

roles: Capulet, Polonius, Brabantio. At the time of Shakespeare's death, he had probably retired from acting and become the business manager of the King's Men. It is to Heminges and his associate Condell that we owe the First Folio edition of Shakespeare's works (1623).

Of Henry Condell's parts only one can be established with certainty: that of the cardinal in John Webster's *The Duchess of Malfi*. In regard to his Shakespearean roles, we are reduced to guesswork. Baldwin believes that he played worthy young gentlemen of the Horatio and Benvolio type. Energetic young men seem to have been played by William Sly: Macduff, Hotspur, Tybalt, and Laertes. We have no confirmation of Baldwin's assumption that Shakespeare wrote to order for him such parts as Claudius, Ford, and Cassius.

What of Shakespeare the actor? In the dialogue *Historia Histrionica* (1699), one of the interlocutors reports having heard that Shakespeare "was a much better Poet than Player." Surely no one will doubt this. Nicholas Rowe, in the introduction to his Shakespeare edition of 1709, tells us that Shakespeare played the Ghost in *Hamlet*. All of Rowe's investigations gleaned only the meager information "that the top of his Performance was the Ghost in his own *Hamlet*." This exhausts our sources; the rest is hypothesis. Baldwin believes that Shakespeare played dignified parts, short but crucial for the action; among these roles he numbers the Ghost, but also King Duncan, the Duke in *All's Well that Ends Well*, and perhaps Adam in *As You Like It*. Since

Shakespeare probably directed most of his own plays, these short roles enabled him to supervise rehearsals.

Shakespeare the director is mentioned in the remark that Lowin "had his Instructions from M. Shakespear himself." Johannes Rhenanus, physician of Cassel, who visited London at the turn of the seventeenth century, believed that not the least reason for the excellence of the English theatre was that the dramatists themselves instructed the actors. In the preface to his German adaptation of *Lingua,* an English play, Rhenanus wrote (8) in 1613, "As for the actors, they (as I have noted in England) are instructed daily as though at school; even the most prominent actors must permit themselves to be instructed in their parts by the poets, and this is what endows a well-written comedy with life and grace. Thus it is no wonder that the English comedians (I speak of the practiced ones) are more excellent than others." John Aubrey wrote, ca. 1681, that Ben Jonson "was never a good Actor, but an excellent Instructor." Shakespeare, too, must be regarded as such an "instructor," a *didaskalos* in the Greek sense. Of course, all trace of his activity as a director has been effaced, and Flatter's attempts (12) to detect Shakespeare's "Producing Hand" through the commas and periods in the Folio are of doubtful value, for the ways of printers at the time of James I are a very shaky foundation for a theory. Nevertheless, a stage direction in the pirated editions or in the First Folio sometimes discloses a director's "gimmick," such as we have seen in the quartos of *Romeo and*

Juliet. We still see the hand of Shakespeare the director in the sentries' scene in *Antony and Cleopatra*, IV. iii, where he notes that the soldiers "place themselves in euery corner of the Stage," whence they hear the mysterious notes of the oboes from below: "Musicke of the Hoboyes is vnder the Stage." When Volumnia implores the defiant Coriolanus, a stage direction at the end of her speech says, "He holds her by the hand, silent." What could be simpler yet more eloquent than this reaching out for the (fatal) maternal hand and this pause of silence? And there is still another silence, far more terrible, when Macduff hears the news that his wife has been murdered and at first finds no words for his pain, so that Malcolm cries out in terror:

What, man! ne'er pull your hat upon your brows;
Give sorrow words.

It is certain that as Jacob Isaacs (28) has shown, this silence and Macduff's gesture of drawing his hat down over his brows were Shakespeare's doing.

The female roles were played by apprentices assigned to the different actors for instruction. They learned their trade from the masters, as other apprentices learned theirs from the blacksmith or cabinetmaker. We know the names of some of these apprentices and the masters under whom they were trained. Robert Gough (Goffe) was apprenticed to Thomas Pope, and was possibly the first Juliet. James Sands spent his apprenticeship under Augustine Phillips. Alexander Cooke and John Rice were assigned to John Heminges. Nicholas Tooley trained

77

under Burbage. These are only a few of the young men who created Shakespeare's female roles. It is hazardous to connect specific roles with specific apprentices. It would be risky even to insist that when an apprentice grew up he played the same type of role as his master.

10. The Style of Acting

WE KNOW little about the style of the Shakespearean actors and it is doubtful whether we shall ever
know much more. Our problem could be stated very
simply in one question: how did Richard Burbage
act? When we sift the scanty source material concerning this actor, who for the first time played some
of the most famous parts in world literature, we cannot help being reminded of Schiller's remark that
the actor's art "passes swiftly and without a trace."
Let us take Hamlet's instructions to the players as
a starting point. Burbage was Shakespeare's first
Hamlet, and we may feel sure that he was not guilty
of the mistakes for which Hamlet criticized other
actors. When he warns the players who are visiting
Elsinore not to mouth their lines but to speak the
speech trippingly on the tongue, Burbage-Hamlet is
no doubt characterizing his own style. It is not likely
that he sawed the air with his hands or tore a passion
to tatters, that he split the ears of the groundlings,
or, in general, let himself be carried away by the
whirlwind of his passion. Hamlet's, and no doubt
Shakespeare's, ideal of an actor was one who acquires
and begets a temperance and never o'ersteps the
modesty of nature. He must not overact nor must
he be "too tame," and in these respects Burbage
must have been a master, or else Shakespeare would
scarcely have written these lines for him. "Suit the
action to the word, the word to the action": Burbage

must have achieved this harmony of word and gesture.

Burbage apparently painted in his free time. In 1615 there appeared an anonymous character sketch entitled "An Excellent Actor." Since it describes an actor with a taste for painting, presumably the portrait refers to Burbage. In any case we are told that this excellent actor "doth not striue to make nature monstrous, she is often seene in the same Scaene with him, but neither on Stilts nor Crutches; and for his voice tis not lower then the prompter, nor lowder then the Foile and Target." In short: "By a full and significant action of body, he charmes our attention." All this would fit the Burbage whom we have reconstructed from Hamlet's words to the players.

When Burbage died on May 20, 1619, a number of epitaphs and elegies appeared. The finest obituary was that by the Earl of Pembroke, who a week after the actor's death could not yet bring himself to visit the theatre with other noblemen, "so soone after the loss of my old acquaintance Burbadg." The most detailed description of Burbage is to be found in Richard Flecknoe's *A Short Discourse of the English Stage* (1664), a late document, written forty-five years after the actor's death. Flecknoe himself cannot have seen Burbage on the stage, and we do not know how reliable his information was. He called Burbage "a delightful Proteus, so wholly transforming himself into his Part, and putting off himself with his Cloathes, as he never (not so much as in the Tyring-house), assum'd himself again until the play was done . . ." Flecknoe praised Burbage's voice and compared him to "an excellent singer, who knows

80

all his Graces, and can artfully vary and modulate his Voice . . . an excellent Orator (animating his words with speaking, and Speech with Action)." Even in his silences "he was an excellent Actor still, never falling in his Part when he had done speaking; but with his looks and gesture, maintaining it still unto the heighth." Certain scholars have combined Flecknoe's testimony with Hamlet's "to hold as 'twere the mirror up to nature," and inferred that Burbage practiced a kind of psychological realism. This I regard as a fallacy despite Marvin Rosenberg's arguments (39).

The mere fact that, while Burbage played Macbeth, an adolescent impersonated Lady Macbeth seems to me to exclude any possibility of realism. A lad of sixteen could not possibly have played Lady Macbeth realistically. There was only one way to make the figure credible: stylization. And if the young player stylized Lady Macbeth, the adult Burbage must also have stylized. An inconsistency of technique is inconceivable. The adult portrayer of Romeo on the platform of the Theatre and the apprentice disguised as Juliet on the gallery or pavilion roof must be reduced to a common denominator, and this common denominator can only be style. Such stylization did not exclude an emotional reaction on the part of the public any more than the stylization of Mei Lan-fang, the great female impersonator, prevented the Chinese from weeping, or any more than the female roles played by men in the Kabuki Theatre detract from the emotion of Japanese audiences. Thus when we are informed that at a performance of *Othello* (43) in Oxford (1610) the King's

81

Men "moved the audience to tears, not only by their speech, but by their gestures as well" (*In quibus* [*Tragediis*] *non solum dicendo, sed etiam faciendo quaedam lachrymas movebant*), it does not mean that they obtained this effect by the use of a subjective, realistic approach. At this performance in Oxford, one spectator was deeply impressed by the death of Desdemona, "especially when she lay in bed, moving the spectators to pity solely by her face" (*cum in lecto decumbens spectantium misericordiam ipso vultu imploraret*). This report proves only that there were young actors who knew their trade and that the bed in which Desdemona was smothered was placed so close to the audience that every detail of her facial expression could be seen (as would not have been possible in an alcove).

In passing, let us say something of a theatrical form in which the Elizabethan upper classes took great delight: the children's troupes, which not only appeared at Court but also gave public performances at the Blackfriars Playhouse. We can still gain some idea of the enchantment created by these children by recalling the light operas performed by the Wiener Sängerknaben. Originally, the children were trained only to sing in church. Later, they were used for dramatic performances, and first-rank authors such as John Lyly and Ben Jonson wrote plays for them. Some of these choristers later became professional actors: Nathan Field, for example, as a boy had belonged to the Children of the Chapel, and after Shakespeare's death became one of the leading members of the King's Men. It would be hard to imagine that these children played realistically. Field had no difficulty in effecting the transition to professional acting, because he had learned the art of stylization as a boy and continued to practice it as an adult. Stylization is characteristic of all the great epochs of the theatre. The contemporaries of Elizabeth and James I knew perfectly well that their theatre was—theatrical. They surrounded the actors on three sides; they were familiar with the characteristic techniques of the various players in the different repertory theatres; no one had yet thought of illusion and the picture-frame stage. The theatre had not yet fallen from grace. Anyone who took the appearance for reality was an object of ridicule, like the Citizen's Wife in Francis Beaumont's *The Knight of the Burning Pestle.*

Elizabethan actors were trained dancers and acrobats. For good reason the English comedians were known on the Continent as tumblers and employed by princes as such. Balthasar Paumgartner of Nuremberg, who attended performances of Robert Browne's company at the Frankfurt Fair in 1592, wrote to his wife on September 13: "The English comedians have wonderful music and are so skilled at tumbling and dancing that I have never heard nor seen the like." In his description of the Sackville troupe at Frankfurt in 1597, Marx Mangoldt (8) expresses his admiration for the English *Springer:* "I should also praise the tumbler for his high leaps and other things as well. He is courtly in all his ways, in dancing and all his steps. It is a delight to see how smooth his trousers fit . . ."

An English actor also had to be a skilled fencer; otherwise he would have made himself ridiculous in the presence of the aristocratic pupils of Rocco Bonetti, the celebrated fencing master. The combats between Macbeth and Macduff, the duel scene in *Hamlet*, the duels in *Romeo and Juliet*, unlike today's usual stage duel, must have provided great excitement. Here there was scarcely any stylization. But "armies" moved across the stage in formal, conventional groupings. The stage direction to III. x in *Antony and Cleopatra* is enlightening in this respect: "Camidius Marcheth with his Land Army one way ouer the stage, and Towrus the Lieutenant of Caesar the other way: After their going in, is heard the noise of a Sea fight." An Army that came in by one stage door and went out through the other probably consisted of four or five symbolic soldiers and a standard bearer. This, in other words, was epic theatre.

11. Pageantry and Costumes

THE ELIZABETHAN AUDIENCE was fascinated by
processions and pantomime pageants, and the players
catered to this taste. Shakespeare's (and Fletcher's)
Henry VIII made ample use of processional, panto-
mimic elements. The coronation procession in Act
IV, for example, is announced by "a lively flourish of
Trumpets." First came two Judges, then the Lord
Chancellor with the purse and mace. Next enter
choristers singing, the Lord Mayor of London "bearing the mace," a Knight of the Garter wearing "a gilt
copper crown," the Marquess Dorset "bearing a
sceptre of gold, on his head a demi-coronal of gold,"
"with him the Earl of Surrey bearing the rod of
silver with the dove crowned with an earl's coronet."
Then proceed the Duke of Suffolk, his coronet on his
head, bearing a long, white wand, as high steward;
"A canopy borne by four of the Cinqueports; under
it, the Queen in her robe"; "on each side her, the
Bishops of London and Winchester"; "the old Duchess of Norfolk, in a coronal of gold, wrought with
flowers, bearing the Queen's train"; finally, "Certain
Ladies or Countesses, with plain circlets of gold without flowers." As the procession crosses the stage,
from one stage door to the other, two noblemen exchange their observations. In the following scene we
have an example of a dumb show such as had been
common on the English stage since the days of *Gor-
boduc*. Queen Catherine has fallen asleep; a vision appears to her:

Enter, solemnly tripping one after another, six personages, clad in white robes, wearing on their heads garlands of bays, and golden vizards on their faces; branches of bays or palm in their hands. They first congee unto her, then dance; and, at certain changes, the first two hold a spare garland over her head; at which the other four make reverent curtsies. Then the two that held the garland deliver the same to the next two, who observe the same order in their changes, and holding the garland over her head; which done, they deliver the same garland to the last two, who likewise observe the same order; at which, as it were by inspiration, she makes in her sleep signs of rejoicing, and holdeth up her hands to heaven: and so in their dancing vanish, carrying the garland with them. The music continues.

Pericles contains several such dumb shows. And finally, we must mention the ballets that were inserted in several of Shakespeare's plays: the dance of the Amazons in *Timon of Athens* and the dance of the Shepherds and Satyrs in *A Winter's Tale*.

Elizabethan dress, both for weekdays and holidays, is known to us in every detail. Everything that is worth knowing on the subject may be found in Channing Linthicum's book (31). Nevertheless, there is still no thorough study of Elizabethan stage costumes. The players of the time would have been not a little surprised at such neglect; for them the costumes were essential parts of their roles. Foreign observers were always impressed by the richness of their dress. One of these observers was Platter: "The comedians are dressed most expensively and elegantly, for it is the custom in England that when noble lords or knights die, they leave almost their finest clothes to their servants, who, because it is not fitting, do not wear such clothes, but sell them to the comedians for a paltry price." We cannot judge the authenticity of Platter's information. During the Restoration, we hear, the actors sometimes received castoff garments as presents from their aristocratic patrons. When Orazio Busino, chaplain of the Venetian Legation in London, visited the Fortune Playhouse in 1617, he saw a tragedy of which he did not understand a word; but he did not regard the afternoon as a total loss, for he had greatly enjoyed the music and the dances. And above all he had taken pleasure in the "magnificent costumes of the actors." The sumptuousness of the English comedians' costumes was almost proverbial as we can gather from a remark of Johann Olorinus (*Ethnographia Mundi*, Magdeburg, 1613): "Sometimes three different kinds of velvet of different colors must be taken for a doublet / and cut through / so that it can be seen: The collars must be set with pearls / and such is their splendor / that they resemble the English comedians in the Theatre." Hence it is no wonder that when Fynes Moryson saw the English comedians in Frankfurt, he was outraged that this wretched troupe should have no "good Apparell" (or anything else that would have commended it to an Englishman). Balthasar Paumgartner, who was less demanding (he was not an Englishman), declared that the English players were "dressed magnificently and well."

We possess only one contemporary picture that seems to tell us something about the costumes worn by Elizabethan actors. It is a drawing done in 1595 of a scene (I. i. 130) in Shakespeare's *Titus Andronicus*. Dover Wilson (44), who first analyzed this drawing in detail, established its authenticity. We see the captive queen of the Goths on her knees before Titus; behind her stand two of her sons (the third has just been slain); Aaron the Moor is furiously brandishing his sword—strange behavior for a prisoner; Titus holds a *hasta* in his left hand; and behind him are two bodyguards with halberds. The two Roman guards are dressed like Elizabethan soldiers. The bearded Titus, to be sure, wears a Roman costume, with armor and toga. Wilson sees the features of a boy in Tamora and thinks that possibly the Moor was played by Burbage and Titus by Shakespeare. He takes the sketch as proof that the character of Titus Andronicus at least appeared in a "historical" costume on the Elizabethan stage. But one is disturbed by Aaron's straight sword. According to a line in the play (IV. ii. 91) Aaron bore a "scimitar," that is, a curved sword as befits a Moor. I believe that Aaron carried a curved sword on the Elizabethan stage, and this leads me to doubt the value of a sketch showing a straight sword in the hand of a prisoner. Perhaps, then, we should not attach too much importance to Titus' toga.

In *Julius Caesar* Casca speaks of Caesar's "doublet," which supports our belief that the triumvir, like Macbeth and Romeo, was dressed in the contemporary Elizabethan style and that no importance was attached to historical accuracy. If Cleopatra bade

Charmian to "cut her lace," that is, to undo the stays of her corset, it meant that on the Shakespearean stage the attire of the Egyptian Queen did not differ from that of a well-dressed lady of 1600. Cleopatra's dress was no doubt similar in cut to that of the Queen in *Hamlet*, though perhaps brighter colors were used for Egypt than for gloomy Denmark.

Henslowe's inventory (15) of 1598 lists a large number of costumes. Some were intended for definite parts, such as Neptune's costume, "Tamberlanes breches of crymson vellvet," "Tamberlynes cotte, with coper lace." Phaeton had his own costume, though no description of it is given, and the same is true of the poet Tasso and of Robin Hood. Queen Dido and the goddess Juno had their gowns. "Harye the v." wore a "velvet gowne" and a "satten dublet, layd with gowld lace." There was a "yellow leather dublett for a clowne." Shepherds, Roman senators, Templars, and Janizaries were apparently characterized by their costumes. Ghosts had a symbolic dress, "a robe for to go invisibell." The storerooms of the Rose Playhouse also included a costume for Merlin the magician.

The costumes were made of silk, velvet, taffeta, russet, and (very rarely) damask. Gold and silver brocade were also used. A calico dress was reserved for a queen; since this material had to be imported from India, it was very expensive. Most of the costumes were trimmed with laces of gold, silver, or copper. Because Henslowe sometimes states expressly that a certain trimming is only "sylver lace of coper," we may feel certain that when gold or silver lace is listed as such, it was genuine.

As for the colors, the Rose Playhouse possessed doublets of the following colors: one of white satin with taffeta trimming; one "blacke satten dublet, layd thyck wyth blacke and gowld lace," and one of peach color with silver lace. We hear also of a "pynked," dark-red doublet and an orange-colored one with gold lace. Other items in Henslowe's stock were short jerkins with or without sleeves, that were worn over the doublet. A green, black, or red garment of this type was in every case trimmed with silver lace. Some jerkins were of black, white, or "murrey" leather. There were full-length and knee-length cloaks. Henslowe lists a short cloak of black velvet, trimmed with white fur. Another short cloak was of yellow-brown satin and had sleeves. There was a long cloak of purple with silver buttons, another of black velour with broad, black lace trimmings (perhaps for the Prologue); a third of russet was trimmed with copper. Venetian-type breeches, or "Venesyones," are frequently listed. These extended below the knee, and Henslowe possessed a red pair with "sylver lace of coper," another pair peach-colored with copper lace, and a dark-red pair trimmed with gold. The Rose was not so rich in female costumes. In addition to those for Dido and Juno, we also find a woman's dress of "cloth of gowld," one of orange velour with silver trimming, a black velvet dress embroidered with gold, a yellow satin dress "ymbradered with sylk and gowld lace." A "white tafitie sherte with gowlde frenge" was also probably intended for a female part. Henslowe possessed four hoop skirts ("ferdingalles"), gloves, fans, crowns, scepters, suits of armor, swords, and helmets.

90

Elizabethan fashions, like ours, were in constant flux, and it is certain that the actors could not keep up with the swift changes. Moryson writes in his travel book that dress fashions were created for the Court, and that the courtiers abandoned a style as soon as it began to be imitated by the burghers and "the very Stage-players themselues." It has been reckoned that the value of the costumes stocked in an Elizabethan theatre considerably exceeded that of the building. Henslowe's *Diary* (14) indicates the prices. He paid £6.3s. for a black velour dress worn by Mrs. Frankford in Thomas Heywood's *A Woman Killed with Kindness*. Two taffeta dresses cost him £9. A flame-colored silk doublet was acquired for forty-five shillings. A "voivode's" suit cost him £10. A robe of estate cost no less than £19. On the Elizabethan stage the actors were extremely close to the audience, and shabby costumes would have destroyed the illusion.

12. The "Private" Blackfriars Theatre

So FAR we have spoken only of the "public" theatre. However, it was for a "private" theatre that Shakespeare wrote his late "romances": the Blackfriars. The name refers to a Dominican cloister secularized under Henry VIII. In 1576 a theatre was set up in the former monastery by Richard Farrant who had instructed the choir boys of Windsor Chapel, and occasionally produced plays with them for the entertainment of the Queen. Here, noblemen were permitted to attend the rehearsals of Court plays. After a time, the rehearsals became regular performances for which sizable admission fees were charged. After Farrant's death the enterprise would have collapsed if the Earl of Oxford had not taken the choir boys under his wing. William Hunnis and Henry Evans were appointed directors of the theatre, and John Lyly, the successful author of *Euphues,* was made chief playwright. Lyly wrote *Alexander and Campaspe* and *Sapho and Phao* for this troupe, whose subsequent destinies we shall not follow.

In 1596 James Burbage was seeking a theatre building, centrally situated and protected from the inclement weather. He chose Blackfriars, which in addition to its favorable situation enjoyed extraterritorial privileges that protected it from the rigors of the puritanical aldermen. Burbage purchased the former refectory building. It is not certain what part of it he transformed into a theatre, whether the ground floor or the second story. In any event, the alterations were made "with great charge and trouble." In earlier years, the second floor had served as a meeting hall for Parliament, and it seems plausible that the Parliament room may have been used for the theatrical performances. The great hall on the ground floor also might have lent itself to dramatic productions. A third possibility would be a combination of the two floors; this would have given Burbage a considerable elevation for both stage and auditorium. "With great charge and trouble" may refer to a drastic alteration of this sort. Documents tell us nothing about the height of the Blackfriars Playhouse, but Shakespeare's late comedies make it clear that the King's Men could not have dispensed with gallery and flying machines. We do know that the theatre measured 66 feet in length and 46 feet in width. The stage was situated at one end of the hall. Nothing is known of its dimensions, but it is generally assumed that the Blackfriars stage was smaller than those of the "public" theatres. The capacity of the house was also smaller. W. J. Lawrence ventures an estimate of six hundred persons, though he assumes that the hall had three galleries. C. W. Wallace arrived at the same figure. Alfred Harbage speaks of "possibly less than seven hundred." E. K. Chambers thinks it possible that there was only one gallery. The standing pit was done away with, and the whole audience was seated on benches or chairs. When there was no room in the place reserved for the audience, the overflow sat on the stage, and some spectators seem to have chosen the stage even when there was room elsewhere. This fashion began at the Blackfriars and spread to the public theatres.

After completing his alterations, Burbage leased the theatre to a children's troupe directed by Nathaniel Giles and Henry Evans. A group of German travelers attended one of these performances at the Blackfriars in 1602, a visit recorded in Friedrich Gerschow's journal (6):

> Thence we went to one of the children's comedies . . . and thereby hangs a tale: the Queen keeps many young boys who must seriously concern themselves with the art of singing and learn to play all manner of instruments, and study in addition. These boys have their special instructors in all arts, and in particular highly accomplished musicians. In order that they may learn courtly manners, they are obliged to act out a comedy each week . . . Anyone wishing to attend such a performance must pay the equivalent of eight Stralsund shillings, and there are always many people and many honorable women in attendance, because useful arguments and many excellent doctrines are treated, as we were told; all this with [artificial] light, which is very impressive. A whole hour in advance one hears fine instrumental music made by organs, lutes, pandoras, mandores, fiddles, and pipes.

The children's success seriously threatened the adult troupes. Rosencrantz reports in *Hamlet* ii. ii, that the children had compelled the professional actors to seek their bread in the provinces: "there is, sir, an aery of children, little eyases, that cry out on the top of the question, and are most tyrannically clapped for't: these are now the fashion, and so berattle the common stages—so they call them—that many wearing rapiers are afraid of goose-quills, and dare scarce come thither." When Hamlet asks him whether the boys "carry it away," Rosencrantz replies, "Ay, that they do, my lord; Hercules and his load too."—an allusion to the Globe. In 1608 Evans lost his lease, and the King's Men moved into the Blackfriars for the winter season, playing there from November to early May and returning to the Globe in the summer.

Shakespeare wrote a number of plays for this theatre: the "romances" of his late years, *Cymbeline*, *The Winter's Tale, The Tempest*. G. E. Bentley (3) has shown that the new house created new problems; special plays were needed for the exacting audience of this "intimate" theatre. It was the "Theatre of a Coterie" (Harbage), for the lower classes were automatically excluded by the high prices. Here greater refinement was required. The courtiers of James I differed from those of Elizabeth; they demanded sophisticated fare, and the playbills soon showed morbid tendencies. Financially, the King's Men were very successful. In one winter at the Blackfriars they took in more than twice what they could earn in a summer at the larger Globe. The future belonged to this exclusive type of playhouse, which anticipated the Restoration theatre. Shakespeare's last comedies were written for this kind of theatre. *Cymbeline* may still have been completed in London; *The Winter's Tale* and *The Tempest* were surely written in Stratford. Do these plays show traces of the new stage? Had the stage form, in contrast to the theatre form, changed in comparison to the public theatre? These questions are still unanswered, for we know very little about the Blackfriars. Nevertheless, let us attempt to visualize how one play, *The Tempest*, was staged at the Black-friars.

In this theatre artificial light was employed, and the stage cannot have been more than forty-six feet wide. Obviously, there was no "shadow," since the roof of the hall provided the necessary protection against rain. The repertory of the playhouse makes it clear that a place was needed for "above" scenes. We must therefore assume that there was a gallery that could be closed off with curtains. There must also have been two side entrances, stage doors that may have been concealed behind a back cloth, and a center entrance was just as indispensable here as in the public theatres. References to these four entrances are found in Thomas Nabbes' play *Covent Garden* which was written for another private theatre, the Phoenix. In his stage directions Nabbes used the terms "by the right Scene," "by the middle Scene," "by the left Scene," and "Enter . . . in the Balcone."

In view of the reduced area of the stage, presumably the players used not a protruding pavilion but an alcove that could be closed by means of a draw curtain. Since the stage had to be lighted artificially in any case (perhaps by chandeliers), the alcove could also be lighted artificially. The Blackfriars was considerably smaller than the public theatres; hence the alcove scenes were close enough to the audience. There was, no doubt, a trap door in the center of the platform, probably in front of the alcove curtain. It is doubtful whether there was room for smaller traps on the sides, for there were usually spectators sitting on the stage, though we do not know how many.

13. *The First Night of* The Tempest

WE CAN hope to reconstruct the performance of
The Tempest at the Blackfriars only if we follow
the stage directions of the First Folio (which were
probably written by Shakespeare himself), and ignore the additions of modern editors. When Arthur
Quiller-Couch and John Dover Wilson (37) prepared their reading edition of *The Tempest*, they
were very liberal with stage directions. We must ignore these editorial additions and consult only the
Folio, which opens with the stage direction "A tem-
pestuous noise of thunder and lightning heard." This,
of course, could be produced on the Blackfriars
stage, while the editors' addition, "The waist of a
ship is seen, seas breaking over it," calls for technical
equipment such as that used in the 1955 production
of *The Flying Dutchman* in Bayreuth. It is quite safe
to assume that, at the Blackfriars, the shipwreck
scene was rendered solely by sound effects and the
agitation of the crew and passengers. The two doors
led to the deck of the ship, and some of the orders
may have been given from above—that is, from the
gallery over the alcove. There must have been a certain measure of realism, for one authentic stage
direction says "Enter mariners wet." Otherwise, the
words of the Chorus at the beginning of the third act
of *Pericles* are applicable:

> In your imagination hold
> This stage the ship, upon whose deck
> The sea-tost Pericles appears to speak.

In the second scene Prospero and Miranda step out of the alcove (in the Globe it would have been the pavilion), before which there may have stood a moss bank. (Henslowe, we recall, possessed two such properties.) We shall probably never know whether Ariel first appeared on the gallery, through the center from the alcove, or through one of the side doors. I do not believe that a cave-like piece was used for Caliban's first entrance, for it would have been superfluous in Caliban's later scenes. The monster comes crawling in through one of the doors and goes out in the same way, while Prospero and Miranda withdraw behind the alcove curtains. Then Ariel comes in, followed by Ferdinand, through the entrance that has not been used by Caliban. Shakespeare's stage direction says that Ariel is "invisible" as he moves about before the Prince, "playing and singing." Possibly, Ariel wore a special costume that was supposed to make him invisible—a convention recognized by the audience. Henslowe's wardrobe, we noted, included "a robe for to go invisibell." Later, Prospero and his daughter enter from the alcove, into which they withdraw with Ferdinand at the end of Act I, while Ariel hurries off through one of the side doors, "by the right Scene" or "by the left Scene," as Nabbes would have said.

The Tempest is divided into acts in the Folio, as are the two other late comedies. We have learned from Gerschow's report that musical offerings were a traditional specialty of the Blackfriars, at least as long as the young choristers, who were trained as musicians, played there; it is conceivable that the adult actors preserved this tradition and filled the intervals between the acts of Shakespeare's romances with a musical program.

In Wilson's and Quiller-Couch's edition the second act opens with the stage direction: "A forest glade in another part of the Island. King Alonso lies upon the turf, his face buried in the grass: Gonzalo, Adrian, Francisco, and others stand about him: Sebastian and Antonio converse apart in low mocking tones." Such a tableau would have been possible only if there were an act curtain. At the Blackfriars Playhouse the above-mentioned persons entered through one door (when the music stopped), the King in the lead, Gonzalo right behind him. The King's mien expresses his dejection, and Gonzalo opens the act by bidding Alonso to "be merry." At the end of the first scene all the courtiers go out through one of the doors and through the other Caliban enters "with a burden of wood." Distant thunder is heard. After the clown scene in the center of the stage, Trinculo, Stephano, and Caliban go out by one of the stage doors.

After a musical interlude, Ferdinand comes in through one of the doors "bearing a log." Miranda appears to him from the alcove. Prospero observes the ensuing scene from the alcove, through a gap in the curtain. At the end of the scene Miranda goes out by one door and Ferdinand by the other; Prospero disappears into the alcove. For the second scene Quiller-Couch and Wilson again imagined a tableau impossible for the Blackfriars: the three rogues are sitting outside the entrance to a cave, drinking. Actually, they must have come in through one of the doors. Ariel, "invisible," overhears the scene in which the murder of Prospero is plotted. Then he lures the trio off the stage with his tabor and pipe. Alonso and his train come in through the opposite door and there begins the banquet scene, for which Shakespeare, since he himself was no longer directing, may have sent detailed instructions from Stratford. Strange, solemn music is heard. Prospero, invisible to the others, appears on the gallery. "Enter several strange shapes, bringing a banquet; and dance about it with gentle actions of salutation; and, inviting the king, &c. to eat, they depart." The trap was not used. The dancing appears to better advantage if the spirits come in and go out through the door. Probably, the banquet was set down in the middle of the platform, leaving the trap in front of the alcove free. It is out of this trap door, behind the table, that Ariel no doubt appeared, dressed "like a harpy," amid thunder and lightning. He has great wings with which he claps on the table "and, with a quaint device, the banquet vanishes." Here we have a mechanical device known as a *secret* in the medieval French theatre: the food vanishes, but not the table, for after Ariel has disappeared through the trap door, amid thunder, the table is carried out by dancing spirits through one of the doors. Ariel's disguise as a harpy is not his only change of costume. In i. ii he has appeared "like a water-nymph," and in iv. i he will have to change again to take the part of Ceres in the masque.

The fourth act most likely began in the alcove, for this gained valuable space for the masque. Iris comes in on foot through one of the doors, Ceres (the disguised Ariel) through the other. As for Juno, the stage direction in the Folio says expressly that she "descends." Thus the Blackfriars must have been equipped with a device for such divine apparitions in a "cloud car." Any attempt to describe this device would be idle speculation: we have nothing to go on but Nicola Sabbattini's *Pratica*. In the masque interlude, reapers appear and join the nymphs to perform a graceful dance. The merry mood is suddenly shattered by Prospero's dark thoughts. "Prospero starts suddenly," and the dancers depart hesitantly "to a strange, hollow, and confused noise." Prospero, Miranda, and Ferdinand probably watched the dance from the alcove, which at this point perhaps was furnished with the chairs and table required in Act v. Then the lovers must have gone out through the center exit, leaving Prospero alone with Ariel. Ariel appears later "with glistering apparel," which he hangs on a tree. This is the first that we hear of a tree, and it is quite conceivable that the tree had been on the stage since i. ii, to provide the exotic color demanded by the "desert island." Later, the spirits appear "in shape of dogs and hounds" to harass the trio. Prospero and Ariel probably looked on from the gallery.

After another musical interlude Prospero, "in his magic robes," and Ariel step forth from the alcove curtain to cast a spell on the courtiers that will hold them fast within the magic circle. Later, Prospero draws the curtain aside and Miranda and Ferdinand are discovered playing chess. After all except Prospero have gone out through the doors, he speaks the Epilogue.

This reconstruction has shown that *The Tempest*

was performed at the Blackfriars under essentially the same conditions as *Romeo and Juliet* at the public theatre. In other words, the King's Men simply moved their winter *mise en scène* to the Globe in summer, where they operated with a pavilion instead of an alcove, but could otherwise use the same "book." And this would have been only logical. We have no record of a performance of *The Tempest* at the Globe. But we do know that in 1611 Simon Forman saw at the Globe performances of *Cymbeline* and *The Winter's Tale*, two comedies that Shakespeare had written primarily for the Blackfriars. We may then assume that *The Tempest* was also included in the Globe's repertory.

14. The Court Masques

THE TEMPEST was produced twice at Court, first
on the evening of November 1, 1611, in Whitehall before James I, and then in the season of 1612/13 as
part of the revels celebrating the marriage of Princess
Elizabeth to the Elector Palatine. Since 1605 the
architect Inigo Jones had been introducing the scenic
elements of the Italian stage into the Court masques.
He had brought the monoscenic stage of illusion,
first the static and later the dynamic variety, to
Whitehall, and the English aristocracy and foreign
diplomats expressed their amazement at the scenic
surprises that could hitherto have been seen only in
Florence and Mantua. For Ben Jonson's *Masque of
Blackness* (1605), Jones had designed a seascape
with moving waves tossing a concave mother-of-pearl
shell. For the *Masque of Beauty* (1608), he had exhibited an "Island floating on a calme water," with
the "throne of Beauty" in the middle. In the *Masque
of Queens* (1609), there was even an *à-vista* scene
change from "an ugly Hell" to the House of Fame.
In 1611, when *The Tempest* was first produced at
Court, Jones created the stage sets for the *Masque
of Oberon*. In the course of the masque a dark rocky
landscape, surrounded by trees, was transformed before the spectator's eyes into the transparent façade
of a palace.

Did the staging of these masques influence the
staging of the plays produced at Court? Would an
audience that had just seen the illusionistic stage of

succession with its perspective paintings used in a masque have been content to see a play by Shakespeare or Fletcher performed on the old polyscenic stage of juxtaposition? We have no proof that Jones had anything to do with the Court productions of the plays belonging to the repertory of the public theatres. But we do know that the same office supervised the performance both of masques and of plays and that the same artisans prepared the stage for both. Should we not, therefore, assume that some of the artistic principles governing the production of the masques affected the staging of the plays? The documents provide no answer, but it seems worth while to call attention to a question that has hitherto not even been raised.

At the time of the wedding celebration in 1613, when *The Tempest* had its second performance at Court, Campion's *The Lords' Masque* was also produced. On this occasion the lower part of the stage represented "a Wood in prospettive, the innermost part being of releave or whole round, the rest painted." On the left side of the stage there was a cave; on the right, a thicket. (The subsequent transformations of this tableau do not concern us here.) It seems quite conceivable that on this occasion *The Tempest* was produced with a similar décor; in other words, that the King's Men played on a prosceniumframe stage with a cave for Caliban, grass mats and palm trees to bring out the exotic atmosphere of the island, and a rocklike built piece hollowed out to provide a cell for Prospero. However, I do not believe that the producers went so far, in the opening scene, as to roll a three-dimensional ship on stage (although that would not have been difficult for the stage technicians of the time, since ships had already been used in the medieval mystery plays). Again we are in the realm of speculation, but it seems more than likely that the shipwreck scene was deleted at Court: it smacks too much of public theatre and is totally superfluous from the dramatic standpoint. It is made sufficiently clear in the ensuing scenes that Alonso, Ferdinand, et al. have been shipwrecked.

15. The Audience

A word about the audience concludes this study. The first public performances of plays in London were held at inns: the Saracen's Head, the Red Lion, the Bell, the Bull, or the Cross Keys. The Lord Mayor and his aldermen had no liking for these places, and if they are to be believed (although persons hostile to the arts deserve no credence), only the scum of humanity gathered there: "theeves, horse-stealers, whoremongers, cozeners, cony-catching persons, practicers of treason, and such other like." When, in consequence of the Common Council's severe restrictions on theatrical activity, Burbage built his Theatre in a northern suburb, the city fathers maintained the same attitude toward the pilgrims to Shoreditch. One cannot contest the presence of undesirable elements, but the scale of admissions suggests that members of all classes were expected. "If a spectator wishes to stand below," Platter tells us, "he pays only one English penny, but if he wishes to sit down [in the third gallery], he is let in through a door and pays another penny; but if he wishes to sit on cushions in the best place [first or second gallery], where he not only sees everything but can also be seen, he pays an additional penny at another door. And since food and drink are distributed during the comedy, he may also take refreshment for his money."

There are various opinions on the capacity of a typical Elizabethan theatre. De Witt estimated that the Swan could seat 3,000 persons. This was probably an exaggeration. Alfred Harbage (19) computed a capacity of 2,344 for the Fortune, though of course there is no reason to suppose that the house was always sold out. The fluctuating receipts at the Rose, entered by Henslowe in his Diary, show that in the year 1595 not much more than an average of 1,000 persons attended the theatre in an afternoon. An impressionistic account of the crowd and bustle at the popular Fortune Playhouse is to be found in *The Roaring Girl*, by Middleton and Dekker. At the beginning of the play Sir Alexander describes the audience to his friends:

Stories of men and women, mix'd together,
Fair ones with foul, like sunshine in wet weather;
Within one square a thousand heads are laid,
So close that all of heads the room seems made.

Among them he sees a pickpocket, who "leers with hawk's eyes for his prey." But most had come to witness the spectacle:

The very floor, as 't were, waves to and fro,
And, like a floating island, seems to move
Upon a sea bound in with shores above.

The presence of women in the audience is attested by numerous sources, not only by the Puritans in whose opinion no one went to a theatre to see a play. Italian visitors, such as Orazio Busino who visited the Fortune in 1617, were particularly astonished to see men and women sitting so unceremoniously side by side. Father Busino (9) was also surprised to see "such a crowd of nobility so very well arrayed that they looked like so many princes, listening as silently and soberly as possible." The Earls of Essex and Southampton were sometimes seen in the public theatre with their retinues. The boxes nearest the stage in the lowermost story were set aside for the nobility; these were the "Lords' Rooms." (In De Witt's sketch these "gentlemens roomes" are designated as "orchestra.") Here the admission fee was 12*d*. When the custom of sitting on the stage was taken over from the private theatres, the "twelve-penny room" lost its social value, and the lords and those who aped them sat on the stage. The Lords' Room was now transformed into a kind of trysting place, and the price seems to have been cut in half. Ben Jonson refers occasionally to the "six-penny mechanicks" who busied themselves with harlots in the dark corners of these loges.

Sometimes a "gull" showed himself in the gallery and was ridiculed in an epigram. It goes without saying that no Elizabethan Martial took an interest in those who behaved properly at the theatre. Only the deviations from the norm have been immortalized, particularly the witless gallant who, though dressed in the latest style, had no idea how to conduct himself. Jonson gives us a magnificent example of such "eminence of clothes, not understandings" in the prologue to *Cynthia's Revels,* a play written for the Blackfriars. Jonson's dandies remind us of Molière's marquises a century later. No sooner does the gull enter than he begins to be difficult, cursing as he throws his coins into the "gatherer's" box. Then he sits down "like a peece of Ordnance" on a "three-footed stoole" on the stage and begins a soliloquy to

which his neighbors are compelled to listen. He has
three kinds of tobacco with him and swears that if he
did not smoke he could not bear the foul smell of the
place. He finds the music hideous, the play abomina-
ble, and has no kind word for the players. Among
these "gallants" there were would-be critics who
would pass judgments on the play, though the latest
fashions and the prices of satin and velour were the
sum of their knowledge. Jonson tells us of one of these
"Caprichious gallants" with "more beard than
brain," who twirled his mustache and assured those
about him that the old play *Jeronimo* was the best in
Europe. Of course, it must be admitted that Ben Jonson judged the audiences solely by their education.
For the English theatre Jonson's own folio edition of
his *Works* was a fall from innocence. He gave the
stage a literary tone. He was always ready with a
programmatic manifesto. The audience should be educated for such "higher pleasures" as the unities of
time and action. Jonson paid for his pedagogic zeal
with a loss of universal appeal. The premiere of his
Sejanus at the Globe in 1603 was a fateful occur-
rence: the audience split into two camps; the "multi-
tude" rejected the play, only the educated ap-
plauded. But the educated sometimes left the poet in
the lurch, and even at Court he ultimately ran into
difficulties when the audience preferred the "Omni-
potent Designe" of Inigo Jones to the humanistic
baggage which Jonson regarded as the substance of
his masques.

In his wiser moods, to be sure, Jonson admitted
that "the people generally" were a thoroughly recep-
tive audience. The backbone of the Elizabethan the-

atre consisted of the merchants and artisans, whose intellectual level and taste has been described by Louis B. Wright (47) in his brilliant study of Elizabethan middle-class culture. Wright's investigations show that the foundations for the swift rise of the English bourgeoisie in the eighteenth century were laid during the reign of Queen Elizabeth. By the end of the Tudor period the burghers were becoming aware of their power and developing the ideals of the third estate. These burghers were not wholly taken up by their trades; a certain Renaissance curiosity stirred within them, and they found time in which to educate themselves. C. J. Sisson was mistaken in regarding the grocer's family caricatured by Beaumont as "representative spectators."

Shakespeare lived in the finest harmony with his audience. Unlike Jonson, he was never intolerant toward it; he took it as he found it. The prologue to *Henry VIII*, one of Shakespeare's last plays, shows his understanding of all types of spectators. Shakespeare wishes to prepare his audience for a solemn tone and promises profit to "those that can pity." But he also welcomes those who had come to see a bit of history translated into images. Even the ones who are chiefly interested in sumptuous processions will not be disappointed. Only people who have come

> to hear a merry bawdy play,
> A noise of targets, or to see a fellow
> In a long motley coat guarded with yellow,
> Will be deceived . . .

The epilogue shows that Shakespeare was indulgent even toward those who, taking the whole very lightly, might have napped for an act or two. He did not divide his audience into social layers; he classified them according to their tastes. In his "most comprehensive soul" (Dryden), in the "infinite breadth of his world stage" (Hegel), every variety of spectator found what he had come for.

Documents

A Dutch Humanist Visits the Swan Theatre

In a letter to his friend, Arend van Buchell, Johannes de Witt described (in Latin) and sketched (not too successfully) the interior of the Swan Theatre in 1596.

In London there are four amphitheatres, beautiful to behold. Their names differ according to their diverse signs. In each of them a different play is exhibited to the audiences every day. Two of the better ones are located on the south bank of the Thames River. Their signs indicate that they are called The Rose and The Swan, respectively. The two others are situated to the north [The Theatre and The Curtain], outside the city limits on the road which starts at the Episcopal Gate, commonly called Bishopgate. There is still a fifth [amphitheatre, the Bear Garden] of a different structure, designed for the baiting of animals. Here are housed, in special cubicles, many bears, bulls, and giant dogs, kept for fighting, offering a most enjoyable entertainment.

To be sure, of all the theatres mentioned the one with the sign of the Swan is the largest and most impressive. It is commonly referred to as the Swan Theatre. It can accommodate 3,000 seated spectators. It is built of flint stone (of which Britain has a copious supply) and supported by wooden columns which are painted so cunningly to resemble marble that it could fool even the experts. The shape of the building reminded me of an ancient Roman structure. I have therefore made the above sketch [see Frontispiece].

Amphiteatra Londinij sunt iv visendae pulcritudinis quae a diversis intersigniis diuersa nomina sortiuntur: in iis varia quotidie scaena populo exhibetur. Horum duo excellentiora vltra Tamisim ad meridiam sita sunt, a suspensis signis ROSA et Cygnus nominata: Alia duo extra vrbem ad septentrionem sunt, via qua itur per Episcopalem portam vulgariter Biscopgat nuncupatam. Est etiam quintum, sed dispari [vsu?] et structura, bestiarum concertationi destinatum, in quo multi vrsi, tauri, et stupendae magnitudinis canes, discretis caueis & septis aluntor, qui [drawing occupies rest of page] ad pugnam adseruantur, iocundissimum hominibus spectaculum praebentes. Theatrorum autem omnium prestantissimum est et amplissimum id cuius intersignium est cygnus (vulgo te theatre off te cijn [off te swan]), quippe guod tres mille homines in sedilibus admittat, constructum ex coaceruato lapide pyrritide (quorum ingens in Britannia copia est) ligneis suffultum columnis quae ob illitum marmoreum colorem, nasutissimos quoque fallere possent. Cuius quidem formam quod Romani operis vmbram videatur exprimere supra adpinxi.

Four-Count Indictment of the Theatre

The following letter written by the Lord Mayor and Aldermen to the Privy Council in 1597 summarizes the puritanical objections against playacting.

The inconueniences that grow by Stage playes abowt the Citie of London.

1. They are a speaciall cause of corrupting their Youth, conteninge nothinge but vnchast matters, lascivious devices, shiftes of Coozenage, & other lewd & vngodly practizes, being so as that they impresse the very qualitie & corruption of manners which they represent, Contrary to the rules & art prescribed for the makinge of Comedies eaven amonge the Heathen, who vsed them seldom & at certen sett tymes, and not all the year longe as our manner is. Whearby such as frequent them, beinge of the base & refuze sort of people or such young gentlement as haue small regard of credit or conscience, drawe the same into imitacion and not to the avoidinge the like vices which they represent.

2. They are the ordinary places for vagrant persons, Maisterles men, thieves, horse stealers, whoremongers, Coozeners, Conycatchers, contrivers of treason, and other idele and daungerous persons to meet together & to make theire matches to the great displeasure of Almightie God & the hurt & annoyance of her Maiesties people, which cannot be prevented nor discovered by the Gouernours of the Citie for that they are owt of the Citees jurisdiction.

3. The maintaine idlenes in such persons as haue no vocation & draw apprentices and other seruantes from theire ordinary workes and all sortes of people from the resort vnto sermons and other Christian exercises, to the great hinderance of traides & prophanation of religion established by her highnes within this Realm.

4. In the time of sickness it is fownd by experience, that many hauing sores and yet not hart sicke

115

take occasion hearby to walk abroad & to recreat themselves by heareinge a play. Whearby others are infected, and them selves also many things miscarry.

A Manager Counts His Theatrical Paraphernalia

In March of 1598, Philip Henslowe, business partner of the Lord Admiral's Men, took an inventory of his set pieces and properties stored in the Rose Theatre. From this document it becomes evident that the Elizabethan stage platform was neither a no man's land nor that wasteland J. C. Adams tried to persuade us to accept in 1942. In 1598, we still have one foot in the tradition of medieval theater.

Item, j rocke, j cage, j tombe, j Hell mought.
Item, j tome of Guido, j tome of Dido, j bedsteade.
Item, viij lances, j payer of stayers for Fayeton.
Item, ij stepells, & j chyme of belles, & j beacon.
Item, j hecfor for the playe of Faeton, the limes dead.
Item, j globe, & j golden scepter; iij clobes.
Item, ij marchepanes, & the sittie of Rome.
Item, j gowlden flece; ij rackets; j baye tree.
Item, j. wooden hatchett; j lether hatchete.
Item, j. wooden canepie; owld Mahemetes head.
Item, j lyone skin; j beares skyne; & Faetones lymes, & Faeton charete; & Argosse heade.
Item, Nepun forcke & garland.
Item, j crosers stafe; Kentes woden leage.
Item, Icrosses head, & raynbowe; j littell alter.
Item, viij viserdes; Tamberlyne brydell; j wooden matook.
Item, Cupedes bowe, quiver; the clothe of the Sone & Mone.

Item, j bores heade & Serberosse iij heades.

Item, j Cadeseus; ij mose banckes, & j snake.

Item, ij fanes of feathers; Belendon stable; j tree of gowlden apelles; Tantelouse tre; jx eyorn targates.

Item, j copper targate, & xvij foyles.

Item, iiij wooden targates; j. greve armer.

Item, j syne for Mother Readcap; j buckler.

Item, Mercures wings; Tasso picter; j helmet with a dragon; j shelde, with iij lyones; j eleme bowle.

Item, j chayne of dragons; j gylte speare.

Item, ij coffenes; j bulles head; and j vylter.

Item, iij tymbrells, j dragon in fostes.

Item, j lyone; ij lyon heades; j great horse with his leages; j sack-bute.

Item, j whell and frame in the Sege of London.

Item, j paire of rowghte gloves.

Item, j poopes miter.

Item, iij Imperial crownes; j playne crowne.

Item, j cauderm for the Jewe.

A Swiss Playgoer in London

Thomas Platter, a young medical student from Basel, visited England from September 18 to October 20, 1599. He recorded in his diary visits to the Globe, then brand-new, and the Curtain.

After lunch, on September 21, [1599], at about two o'clock, I and my party crossed the river. In the playhouse with the thatched roof [the Globe] we saw the tragedy of the first Emperor Julius Caesar very well acted by fifteen players. After the play was done there was, as it is customary, a dance: two dressed in men's clothes and two in women's jigged in astonishing fashion.

On another day, I saw, likewise after lunch, a comedy in a playhouse [the Curtain] not far form our suburban inn, if I remember right, in Bishopsgate.

Here were presented various nationals with whom an Englishman fought in defense of his daughter. He defeated them all except the German, who won the daughter in a dual. Next he sat down with her and, to celebrate his victory, he and his servant got drunk. The servant threw his shoe at his master's head, and both fell asleep. Meanwhile, the Englishman entered the tent [pavilion ?] and abducted the girl, thus outwitting the German also. At the end there were very elegant dances, both of the English and Irish variety.

In the city of London, every day at 2 P.M., two and sometimes even three comedies are given at various places, and where there is the best entertainment, there you'll find the most numerous audience. The actors play on a raised stage, and everybody can well see it all. There are, moreover, special galleries where one stands and sits more conveniently, though one has to pay more for this comfort. For the one who remains standing in the yard below pays only one English penny. If he should want to sit, he has to pass a gate where he pays an additional penny. If he desires to sit on a cushion in the most comfortable place where he can see everything and can also be seen, then he gives another penny at still another gate. While the performance is in progress, food and drinks are served among the people, who may refresh themselves at their own expense.

The actors' costumes are most gorgeous and extremely fashionable. For it is customary in England, when noblemen or knights die, that they bequeath or hand down their most sumptuous clothes to their servants. However, as it is not proper for servants to wear such clothes, they offer them to the players for a small amount.

The Globe Gets a Rival

Philip Henslowe's Rose on the Bankside (1587) could not stand comparison with the handsome newcomer, the Globe (1599). Henslowe (in association with Edward Alleyn) decided to erect a playhouse to the north of the City, a structure which was to surpass the Globe both in size and splendor. Peter Streete, who had built the Globe, was to build the Fortune. The contract between Henslowe-Alleyn and the carpenter dated 1599 has been preserved at Dulwich College. It gives dimensions for the building and the stage, measurements which are not applicable to the Globe.

The frame of the saide howse to be sett square and to conteine ffowerscore foote of lawfull assize everye waie square withoutt and fiftie fiue foote of like assize square everye waie within, with a good suer and stronge foundacion of pyles, brick, lyme and sand bothe without & within, to be wroughte one foote of assize att the leiste aboue the grounde; And the saide fframe to conteine three Stroies in heighth, the first or lower Storie to conteine Twelve foote of lawfull assize in heighth, the second Storie Eleauen foote of lawfull assize in heighth, and the third or vpper Storie to conteine Nyne foote of lawfull assize

in height; All which Storie shall conteine Twelue
foote and a halfe of lawfull assize in breadth
througheout, besides a juttey forwardes in either
of the saide twoe vpper Stories of Tenne ynches of
lawfull assize, with ffower convenient divisions for
gentlemens roomes, and other sufficient and convenient divisions for Twoe pennie roomes, with necearrie
seates to be placed and sett, aswell in those roomes
as througheoute all the rest of the galleries of the
saide howse, and with suchelike steares, conveyances
& divisions withoute & within, as are made & contryved in and to the late erected Plaiehowse on the
Banck in the saide parishe of Ste Saviours called the
Globe; With a Stadge and Tyreinge howse to be
made, erected & settupp within the saide fframe, with
a shadowe or cover over the saide Stadge, which
Stadge shalbe placed & sett, as alsoe the stearecases
of the saide fframe, in such sorte as is prefigured in
a plott thereof drawen, and which Stadge shall conteine in length Fortie and Three foote of lawfull
assize and in breadth to extende to the middle of the
yarde of the saide howse; The same Stadge to be
paled in belowe with good, stronge and sufficyent
newe oken bourdes, and likewise the lower Storie of
the saide fframe withinside, and the same lower
storie to be alsoe laide over and fenced with stronge
yron pykes; And the said Stadge to be in all other
proporcions contryved and fashioned like vnto the
Stadge of the saide Plaie howse called the Globe;
With convenient windowes and lightes glazed to the
saide Tyreinge howse; And the saide fframe, Stadge
and Stearecases to be covered with Tyle, and to

120

haue a sufficient gutter of lead to carrie & convey
the water frome the coveringe of the saide Stadge
to fall backwardes; And also all the saide fframe and
the Staircases thereof to be sufficyently enclosed
withoute with lathe, lyme & haire, and the gentlemens
roomes and Twoe pennie roomes to be seeled with
lathe, lyme & haire, and all the fflowers of the saide
Galleries, Stories and Stadge to be bourded with
good & sufficyent newe deale bourdes of the whole
thicknes, wheare need shalbe; And the saide howse
and other things beforemencioned to be made & doen
to be in all other contritivions, conveyances, fashions, thinge and thinges effected, finished and doen
accordinge to the manner, and fashion of the saide
howse called the Globe, saveinge only that all the
princypall and maine postes of the saide fframe and
Stadge forwarde shalbe square and wroughte palasterwise, with carved proporcions called Satiers to
be placed & sett on the topp of every of the same
postes, and saveinge alsoe that the said Peeter
Streete shall not be chardged with anie manner of
pay[ntin]ge in or aboute the saide fframe howse or
Stadge or any parte thereof, nor rendringe the
walls within, nor seeling anie more or other roomes
then the gentlemens roomes, Twoe pennie roomes
and Stadge before remembred.

The Playhouse Manners of a Gallant

In 1609 appeared Thomas Dekker's pamphlet, *The
Gull's Hornbook,* the sixth chapter of which advises a
gallant how he should behave in a playhouse. The section throws light upon the manners some of the Jacobean

gallants must have exhibited when they planted themselves "on the very rushes" of the stage.

The Theater is your Poets Royal Exchange, vpon which, their Muses (that are now turnd to Merchants) meeting, barter away that light commodity of words for a lighter ware then words, *Plaudities* and the *Breath* of the great *Beast*, which (like the threatnings of two Cowards) vanish all into aire. *Plaiers* are their *Factors*, who put away the stuffe, and make the best of it they possibly can (as indeed tis their parts so to doe). Your Gallant, your Courtier, and your Capten, had wont to be the soundest paymaisters, and I thinke are still the surest chapmen: and these by meanes that their heades are well stockt, deale vpon this comical freight by the grosse: when your *Groundling*, and *Gallery Commoner* buyes his sport by the penny, and like a *Hagler*, is glad to vtter it againe by retailing.

Sithence then the place is so free in entertainment, allowing a stoole as well to the Farmers sonne as to your Templer: that your Stinkard has the selfe same libertie to be there in his Tobacco-Fumes, which your sweet Courtier hath: and that your Carman and Tinker claime as strong a voice in their suffrage, and sit to giue iudgement on the plaies life and death, as well as prowdest *Momus* among the tribe of *Critick*: It is fit that hee, whom the most tailors bils do make roome for, when he comes should not be basely (like a vyoll) casd vp in a corner.

Whether therefore the gatherers of the publique or priuate Playhouse stand to receiue the afternoones rent, let our Gallant (hauing paid it) presently aduance himselfe vp to the Throne of the Stage. I meane not into the Lords roome, (which is now but the Stages Suburbs). No, those boxes, by the iniquity of custome, conspiracy of waiting-women and Gentlemen-Ushers, that there sweat together, and the couetousnes of Sharers, are contemptibly thrust into the reare, and much new Satten is there dambd by being smothred to death in darknesse. But on the very Rushes where the Commedy is to daunce, yea and vnder the state of *Cambises* himselfe must our fethered *Estridge*, like a peece of Ordnance be planted valiantly (because impudently) beating down the mewes and hisses of the opposed rascality.

For do but cast vp a reckoning, what large cummings in are pursd vp by sitting on the Stage. First a conspicuous *Eminence* is gotten; by which meanes the best and most essenciall parts of a Gallant (good cloathes, a proportionable legge, white hand, the Persian lock, and a tollerable beard) are perfectly reuealed.

By sitting on the stage, you haue a signd pattent to engrosse the whole commodity of Censure; may lawfully presume to be a Girder: and stand at the helme to steere the passage of *Scaenes* [;] yet no man shall once offer to hinder you from obtaining the title of an insolent, ouer-weening Coxcombe.

By sitting on the stage, you may (without trauelling for it) at the very next doore, aske whose play it is; and, by that *Quest* of *inquiry*, the law warrants you to auoid much mistaking; if you know not the author, you may raile against him: and peraduenture so behaue your selfe, that you may enforce the Author to know you.

By sitting on the stage, if you be a Knight, you may happily get you a Mistresse: if a mere *Fleet street* Gentleman, a wife: but assure yourselfe by continuall residence, you are the first and principall man in election to begin the number of *We three*.

By spreading your body on the stage, and by being a Justice in examining of plaies, you shall put your selfe into such true *Scaenicall* authority, that some Poet shall not dare to present his Muse rudely vpon your eyes, without hauing first vnmaskt her, rifled her, and discouered all her bare and most mysticall parts before you at a Tauerne, when you most knightly shal for his paines, pay for both their suppers.

By sitting on the stage, you may (with small cost) purchase the deere acquaintance of the boyes: haue a good stoole for sixpence: at any time know what particular part any of the infants present: get your match lighted, examine the play-suits lace, and perhaps win wagers vpon laying tis copper, &c. And to conclude whether you be a foole or a Justice of peace, a Cuckold or a Capten, a Lord Maiors sonne or a dawcocke, a knaue or an vnder-Sheriffe, of what stamp soeuer you be, currant or counterfet, the stage, like time, will bring you to most perfect light, and lay you open: neither are you to be hunted from thence though the Scar-crows in the yard, hoot at you, hisse at you, spit at you, yea throw durt euen in your teeth: tis most Gentlemanlike patience to endure all this, and to laugh at the silly Animals: but if the *Rabble* with a full throat, crie away with the foole, you were worse then a mad-man to tarry by it: for the Gentleman and the foole should neuer sit on the Stage together.

Mary let this obseruation go hand in hand with the rest: or rather like a country-seruingman, some fiue yards before them. Present not your selfe on the Stage (especially at a new play) vntill the quaking prologue hath (by rubbing) got cullor into his cheekes, and is ready to giue the trumpets their Cue that hees vpon point to enter: for then it is time, as though you were one of the *Properties*, or that you dropt out of the *Hangings*, to creepe from behind the Arras, with your *Tripos* or three-footed stoole in one hand, and a teston mounted betweene a fore-finger and a thumbe in the other: for if you should bestow your person vpon the vulgar, when the belly of the house is but halfe full, your apparell is quite eaten vp, the fashion lost, and the proportion of your body in more danger to be deuoured, then if it were serued vp in the Counter amongst the Powltry: auoid that as you would the Bastome. It shall crowne you with rich commendation to laugh alowd in the middest of the most serious and saddest scene of the terriblest Tragedy: and to let that clapper (your tongue) be tost so high that all the house may ring of it: your Lords vse it; your Knights are Apes to the Lords, and do so too: your Inne-a-court-man is Zany to the Knights, and (many very scuruily) comes likewise limping after it: bee thou a beagle to them all, and neuer lin snuffing till you haue scented them: for by talking and laughing (like a Plough-man in a Morris) you heap *Pelion* vpon *Ossa*, glory vpon glory: As first, all the eyes in the galleries will leaue walking after the Players, and onely follow you: the simplest dolt in the house snatches vp your name, and when he meetes you in the streetes, or that you fall into his hands in the middle of a Watch, his word shall be taken for you: heele cry, *Hees such a Gallant*, and you passe. Secondly, you publish your temperance to the world, in that you seeme not to resort thither to taste vaine pleasures with a hungrie appetite: but onely as a Gentleman, to spend a foolish houre or two, because yoe can doe nothing else. Thirdly you mightily disrelish the Audience, and disgrace the Author; mary, you take vp (though it be at the worst hand) a strong opinion of your owne judgment and inforce the Poet to take pitty of your weakenesse, and, by some dedicated sonnet to bring you into a better paradice, onely to stop your mouth.

If you can (either for loue or money) prouide your selfe a lodging by the water-side: for, aboue the conueniencie it brings, to shun Shoulder-clapping, and to ship away your Cockatrice betimes in the morning, it addes a kind of state vnto you, to be carried from thence to the staires of your Playhouse: hate a Sculler (remember that) worse then to be acquainted with one ath' Scullery. No, your Oares are your onely Sea-crabs, boord them, and take heed you neuer go twice together with one paire: often shifting is a great credit to Gentlemen; and that diuiding of your fare wil make the poore watersnaks be ready to pul you in peeces to enjoy your custome: No matter whether vpon landing you haue money or no, you may swim in twentie of their boates ouer the riuer upon *Ticket:* mary, when siluer comes in, remember to pay trebble their fare, and it will make your Flounder-catchers to send more thankes after you, when you doe not draw, then when you doe; for they know, It will be their owne another daie.

Before the Play begins, fall to cardes, you may win or loose (as *Fencers* doe in a prize) and beate one another by confederacie, yet share the money when you meete at supper: notwithstanding, to gul the *Ragga-muffins* that stand aloofe gaping at you, throw the cards (hauing first torne foure or fiue of them) round about the Stage, just vpon the third sound, as though you had lost it: skils not if the foure knaues ly on their backs, and outface the Audience, theres none such fooles as dare take exceptions at them, because ere the play go off, better knaues than they will fall into the company.

Now sir, if the writer be a fellow that hath either epigramd you, or hath had a flirt at your mistris, or hath brought either your feather or your red beard, or your little legs, &c. on the stage, you shall disgrace him worse then by tossing him in a blancket, or giuing him the bastinado in a Tauerne, if, in the middle of his play (bee it Pastoral or Comedy, Morall or Tragedie), you rise with a skreud and discontented face from your stoole to be gone: no matter whether the Scenes be good or no, the better they are the worse do you distast them: and, beeing on your feet, sneake not away like a coward, but salute all your gentle acquaintance, that are spred either on the rushes, or on stooles about you, and draw what troope you can from the stage after you: the *Mimicks* are beholden to you, for allowing them

elbow roome: their Poet cries perhaps a pox go with
you, but care not you for that, theres no musick
without frets.

Mary if either the company, or indisposition of
the weather binde you to sit it out, my counsell is
then that you turne plaine Ape, take vp a rush and
tickle the earnest eares of your fellow gallants, to
make other fooles fall a laughing: mewe at passion-
ate speeches, blare at merrie, finde fault with the
musicke, whew at the childrens Action, whistle at the
songs: and aboue all, curse the sharers, that whereas
the same day you had bestowed forty schillings on
an embroidered Felt and Feather, (scotch-fashion)
for your mistress in the Court, or your punck in the
city, within two houres after, you encounter with
the very same block on the stage, when the haber-
dasher swore to you the impression was extant but
the morning.

To conclude, hoard vp the finest play-scraps you
can get, vpon which your leane wit may most sauour-
ly feede for want of other stuffe, when the *Arcadian*
and *Euphuisd* gentlewomen haue their tongues
sharpened to set vpon you: that qualitie (next to
your shittlecocke) is the onely furniture to a Courtier thats but a new beginner, and is but in his
A B C of complement. The next places that are fild,
after Playhouses bee emptied, are (or ought to be)
Tauernes, into a Tauerne then let vs next march,
where the braines of one Hogshead must be beaten
out to make vp another.

The First Globe on Fire

On June 29, 1613, the roof of the first Globe Theatre
caught fire during the fourth scene of the first act of

.Shakespeare's (and Fletcher's) *Henry VIII,* and within an hour the stately structure was burned to the ground. The following, quoted from Sir Henry Wotton's *Reliquiae Wottonianae,* is a portion of a letter he wrote to his nephew, Sir Edmund Bacon.

I will entertain you at the present with what happened this week at the Bankside. The King's Players had a new play, called *All is True,* representing some principal pieces of the reign of Henry the Eighth, which was set forth with many extraordinary circumstances of pomp and majesty, even to the matting of the stage; the Knights of the Order with their Georges and Garter, the guards with their embroidered coats, and the like—sufficient in truth within awhile to make greatness very familiar, if not ridiculous. Now King Henry, making a masque at the Cardinal Wolsey's house, and certain cannons being shot off at his entry, some of the paper or other stuff wherewith one of them was stopped, did light on the thatch, where being thought at first but an idle smoke, and their eyes more attentive to the show, it kindled inwardly, and ran round like a train, consuming within less than an hour the whole house to the very ground. This was the fatal period of that virtuous fabrick; wherein yet nothing did perish but wood and straw, and a few forsaken cloaks; only one man had his breeches set on fire, that would perhaps have broiled him, if he had not, by the benefit of a provident wit, put it out with bottle ale.

Accommodating Actors as Well as Beasts

In August 1613 Henslowe signed a contract with a carpenter named Gilbert Katherens to dismantle the old

Bear Garden and to erect in its place the Hope Theatre, a building which was to serve both for the performance of plays and the baiting of animals. The trestle stage was to be removable. Hence there were no stage posts to sustain "the heavens." Here is a section of the contract where the carpenter agrees to build a . . .

Plaiehouse fitt & convenient in all things, bothe for players to playe in, and for the game of Beares and Bulls to be bayted in the same, and also a fitt and convenient Tyre house and a stage to carryed or taken awaie, and to stande vppon tressells good, substanciall, and sufficient for the carryinge and bearinge of suche a stage; And shall new builde, erect, and sett vp againe the saide plaie house or game place neere or vppon the saide place, where the saide game place did heretofore stande; And to builde the same of suche large compasse, florme, widenes, and height as the Plaie house called the in the libertie of Parris garden in the said parish of St Savious now is; And shall also builde two stearecasses without and adioyninge to the said Playe house in suche convenient places, as shalbe moste fitt and convenient for the same to stande vppon, and of such largnes and height as the stearecasses of the saide playehouse called the Swan nowe are or bee; And shall also builde the Heavens all over the saide stage, to be borne or carryed without any postes or supporters to be fixed or sett vppon the saide stage, and all gutters of leade needfull for the carryage of all suche raine water as shall fall vppon the same; And shall also make two Boxes in the lowermost storie fitt and decent for gentlemen to sitt in; And shall make the particions betwne the Rommes as they

180

are at the saide Plaie house called the Swan; And to make turned cullumes vppon and over the stage; And shall make the principalls and fore fronte of the saide Plaie house of good and sufficient oken tymber, and no furr tymber to be putt or vsed in the lower most, or midell stories, except the vpright postes on the backparte of the saide stories (all the byndinge joystes to be of oken tymber); The inner principall postes of the first storie to be twelve footes in height and tenn ynches square, the inner principall postes in the midell storie to be eight ynches square, the inner most postes in the vpper storie to be seaven ynches square; The prick postes in the first storie to be eight ynches square, in the seconde storie seaven ynches square, and in the vpper most storie six ynches square; Also the brest sommers in the lower moste storie to be nyne ynches depe, and seaven ynches in thicknes, and in the midell storie to be eight ynches depe and six ynches in thicknes; The byndinge jostes of the firste storie to be nyne and eight ynches in depthe and thicknes, and in the midell storie to be viij and vij inches in depthe and thicknes. Item to make a good, sure, and sufficient foundacion of brickes for the saide Play house or game place, and to make it xiij^{teene} ynches at the leaste above the grounde.

Reading List

1. ADAMS, J. C. *The Globe Playhouse*. Cambridge, Mass., 1942.
2. BALDWIN, T. W. *The Organization and Personnel of the Shakespearean Company*. Princeton, 1927.
3. BENTLEY, G. E. "Shakespeare and the Blackfriars Theatre," *Shakespeare Survey, 1* (1948), 38–50.
4. BETHELL, S. L. "Shakespeare's Actors," *Review of English Studies*, new ser., *1* (1950), 193–205.
5. BINZ, G. "Londoner Theater und Schauspiele im Jahre 1599," *Anglia*, new ser., *10* (1899), 456–64.
6. CHAMBERS, E. K. *The Elizabethan Stage*. 4 vols. Oxford, 1923.
7. ——— *William Shakespeare*. 2 vols. Oxford, 1930.
8. CREIZENACH, W. *Die Schauspiele der englischen Komödianten*. Berlin and Stuttgart, n.d.
9. "Diaries and Despatches of the Venetian Embassy at the Court of King James I, in the Years 1617, 1618," *Quarterly Review, 102* (1857), 398–438.
10. DOVER, K. J. "Greek Comedy," in M. Platnauer, ed., *Fifty Years of Classical Scholarship* (Oxford, 1954), p. 96.
11. FEUILLERAT, A. *Documents Relating to the Office of the Revels in the Time of Queen Elizabeth*. Louvain, Leipzig, and London, 1908.
12. FLATTER, R. *Shakespeare's Producing Hand*. New York, 1948.
13. GRANVILLE-BARKER, H. *Prefaces to Shakespeare, 2* vols. Princeton, 1946.

14. GREG, W. W., ed. *Henslowe's Diary,* 2 vols. London, 1904–08.
15. —— *Henslowe Papers: Being Documents Supplementary to His Diary.* London, 1907.
16. —— *Dramatic Documents from the Elizabethan Playhouses.* Oxford, 1931.
17. —— *The Editorial Problem in Shakespeare.* Oxford, 1942.
18. HARBAGE, A. "Elizabethan Actors," *PMLA, 54* (1939), 685–708.
19. —— *Shakespeare's Audience.* New York, 1941.
20. —— *Theatre for Shakespeare.* Toronto, 1955.
21. HASZLER, K. D. *Die Reisen des Samuel Kiechel.* Stuttgart, 1866.
22. HODGES, C. W. *The Globe Restored.* London, 1953.
23. HOLMES, M. "A New Theory about the Swan Drawing," *Theatre Notebook, 10* (1956), 80–3.
24. HOSLEY, R., ed. *The Tragedy of Romeo and Juliet.* The Yale Shakespeare, New Haven, 1954.
25. HOTSON, L. *Shakespeare versus Shallow.* London, 1931.
26. —— "Shakespeare's Arena," *The Sewanee Review, 61* (1953), 347–61.
27. —— *The First Night of "Twelfth Night."* New York, 1954.
28. ISAACS, J. "Shakespeare as Man of the Theatre," in *Shakespeare and the Theatre,* compiled by members of the Shakespeare Association. London, 1927.
29. JOSEPH, B. L. *Elizabethan Acting.* London, 1951.
30. LAWRENCE, W. J. *The Elizabethan Playhouse and Other Studies,* 2 vols. Stratford-on-Avon, 1912–13.
31. LINTHICUM, M. C. *Costume in the Drama of Shakespeare and His Contemporaries.* Oxford, 1936.
32. NAGLER, A. M. "Sixteenth-Century Continental

Stages," *Shakespeare Quarterly, 5* (1954), 359–70.

33. ——— "Shakespeare's Arena Demolished," *Shakespeare Newsletter, 6* (February 1956), 7.

34. ——— "A Terminology for Sixteenth-Century Stage Forms," *Theatre Research, 1* (1958), in press.

35. ——— "*L'Amico fido* im Uffizien-Theater," *Maske und Kothurn, 4* (1958), in press.

36. PROUTY, C. T. "An Early Elizabethan Playhouse," *Shakespeare Survey, 6* (1953), 64–74.

37. QUILLER-COUCH, A. and WILSON, J. D., eds. *The Tempest.* The New Shakespeare, Cambridge, England, 1921.

38. RIDLEY, M. R., ed. *Antony and Cleopatra.* The Arden Shakespeare, London, 1954.

39. ROSENBERG, M. "Elizabethan Actors: Men or Marionettes?" *PMLA, 69* (1954), 915–27.

40. SHAPIRO, I. A. "The Bankside Theatres: Early Engravings," *Shakespeare Survey, 1* (1948), 23–7.

41. ——— "An Original Drawing of the Globe Theatre," *Shakespeare Survey, 2* (1949), 21–3.

42. TIECK, L. *Der junge Tischlermeister,* in his *Schriften, 28,* Berlin, 1854.

43. TILLOTSON, G. "*Othello* and *The Alchemist* at Oxford in 1610," *The Times Literary Supplement* (July 20, 1933), p. 494.

44. WILSON, J. D. "*Titus Andronicus* on the Stage in 1595," *Shakespeare Survey, 1* (1948), 17–24.

45. ———, ed. *King Henry V.* The New Shakespeare, Cambridge, England, 1947.

46. ———, ed. *Antony and Cleopatra.* The New Shakespeare, Cambridge, England, 1950.

47. WRIGHT, L. B. *Middle-Class Culture in Elizabethan England.* Chapel Hill, 1935.

Index